Bountiful Harvest

From Land to Table

Bountiful Harvest

From Land to Table

BETTY LADUKE

White Cloud Press
In association with The Ashland Food Co-op
Ashland, Oregon

White Cloud Press titles may be purchased for educational, business, or sales promotional use. For information, please write:

Special Market Department
White Cloud Press
PO Box 3400, Ashland, OR 97520
Website: www.whitecloudpress.com

Art credits: All art and photos from the personal collection of Betty LaDuke. Cover image: Flower Harvest #4, 2014; p. i, Awakening, 2009; p. vii, Grape Planting, 2015; p. viii, Holly Hock Harvest, 2011; p. x, Grain Medley, 2009; p. xiv, Oregon Cherry Harvest, 2009; back cover, Zinnia Harvest: Morning, Noon, Afternoon, 2014.

Cover and interior design by Christy Collins Medley, C Book Services

Printed in South Korea

16 17 18 19 20   10 9 8 7 6 5 4 3 2 1

Library of Congress Cataloging-in-Publication Data

LaDuke, Betty, author.

Bountiful harvest : from land to table / by Betty LaDuke ; foreword by Bonnie Laing-Malcolmson.

    pages cm

Includes bibliographical references and index.

ISBN 978-1-940468-26-6 (pbk. : alk. paper)

1. Agriculture in art. 2. Farmers in art. 3. LaDuke, Betty. I. Title.

N8217.A49L33 2015

759.13--dc23

                        2015031958

Dedication

To the "Hands in the Dirt" people:
The inspiration for *Bountiful Harvest.*

Table of Contents

Foreword

Born in the Bronx, New York, to Russian and Polish immigrant parents, Betty LaDuke knew by the age of nine that she would be an artist. Now in her eighties, she remains actively engaged in an artistic practice inspired by the lives of working men and women in developing countries, and, in *Bountiful Harvest*, of working men and women of southern Oregon.

In this rich work of art and stories—told by LaDuke and the subjects of her farm to table paintings—we learn of her study of art as a young woman, first in the United States and then in Mexico. Her Mexico experience whet LaDuke's appetite for travel and seed her lifelong devotion to world cultures. During three years in Mexico, she met artists Rufino Tamayo, Diego Rivera, and David Alfaro Siqueiros, whose dedication to an art representing indigenous working people continues to influence LaDuke's output. Like the Mexican muralists, her early paintings drew upon the modeled forms and earth tones of European Cubism and Expressionism. And like the muralists, her style evolved to embrace the intense colors and flattened, pattern-rich composition of native art and craft.

Her most recent series, *Bountiful Harvest*, the main subject of the book you hold in your hands, celebrates Oregon's agricultural bounty and the workers who plant, tend, and harvest it. Whether depicting laborers in vineyards, orchards, or fields, her bright colors and shaped wooden panels energize her compositions and reflect the dignity of those who sow and reap on Oregon's fertile farmland.

LaDuke settled in Ashland, Oregon in 1964 to teach in the Art Department at Southern Oregon University (then Southern Oregon College). LaDuke travelled alone to India for a month in 1972. Thereafter her extensive travels took her almost exclusively to developing countries in Africa, Latin America, and Southwest Asia. LaDuke has a special interest in the condition of women in the countries she visits, as well as in agrarian workers, craftsmen, and tradespeople who supply the food and products that allow their cultures to develop. She spends countless hours sketching from life, and each trip leads to the production of a series of works reflecting the lives of the people she has visited.

The artist travels abroad less frequently now, and her most recent series featured in this book is rooted closer to home, with Oregon's Latino farm workers and the diverse food crops they cultivate providing fertile subject matter for her shaped plywood panels. Bountiful Harvest is especially pertinent as the Pacific Northwest's Latino population is increasing and controversy over the politics of immigration continues. The subject enables the artist to celebrate and champion her worldview right at home. LaDuke says about hours spent in the fields:

As I paint, I connect with Fry Family Farm workers Raul, Alejandro, Juan, Felix, Rudolfo, or Popo as they bend and kneel to harvest long rows of kale, spinach, squash, cherry tomatoes, sweet peppers, chili peppers, parsley, radishes, and berries. . . . Sometimes in the orchards, as workers climb ladders and empty buckets into bins, they pause to glance at the sketches I make of them. Some approve, "Que bien!" Some wonder, "Why not a camera for better, faster results?" I enjoy our brief dialogues and interactions. I'm especially pleased when the panels featuring local agriculture are on public display in their communities, and the dialogue broadens from the enjoyment of bright colors to the meaning of the work that brings us fresh, local food. . . . The people that inspired my art as a young student living in Mexico, are the very same people that inspire my art now. What was once very far away and different had become close and familiar.[1]

Throughout her career, LaDuke's art has embraced a style and content reminiscent of the American Regionalism espoused during the time of the Great Depression. Exaggerated, caricatured form and heightened color are used expressively to portray the working class.

---

1. From Betty LaDuke, *Bountiful Harvest,* pp. 31-31, 102.

However, LaDuke's global view reaches far beyond the chauvinism of American Regionalism fostered by artists such as Thomas Hart Benton, Grant Wood, and John Steuart Curry. Unlike the Regionalists, she doesn't glorify the strength of workers as symbols of American superiority. Rather, she tells the workers' stories through an art with broad common appeal, bright color, texture, and imagery that simply and directly presents the activities she originally sketched in the fields. The pure color and rhythmic pattern she employs reflect the folk art traditions of the countries she has spent her life visiting. The repeated shapes of leaves, vines, and fruit echo texture and patterns associated with the world's indigenous arts. LaDuke's panels evoke textiles, carvings, and painted decorative objects from Mexico and Guatemala, Mali and Eritrea, aboriginal Australia and Papua New Guinea.

LaDuke's work is illustrative and documentary, political and spiritual. It is not an art for art's sake like Abstract Expressionism, Pop Art, and Minimalist movements that reigned supreme during the artist's formative years. From 1953 through the 1970s, LaDuke claimed a position cognizant of, but outside the dominant spectrum of modern art, even though stylistic nods to artists like Francis Bacon, Willem DeKooning, and Ben Shaun are evident.

LaDuke's sixty-five year retrospective exhibition mounted in 2013 at the Schneider Museum of Art at Southern Oregon University elegantly demonstrated the clear progression of the artist's vision away from contemporary art movements. It proved that while she was always informed about current styles and ideas, she consciously and consistently chose a different, more narrative path—one that was and remains mostly peripheral to mainstream aesthetics. LaDuke's has always been an art of cause and conscience. Her work asks the viewer to value and celebrate the beauty of other cultures, while recognizing humanity's enduring hardships. In 2009, she wrote that her images, "(both personal and political, past and present), . . . bridge people as well as continents. We are one."

–BONNIE LAING-MALCOLMSON, THE ARLENE AND HAROLD SCHNITZER
  CURATOR OF NORTHWEST ART, PORTLAND ART MUSEUM

Preface

I am an artist with pen and sketchbook for shovel and earth. My seeds are the sketches I create of agricultural workers at farms, orchards, and vineyards as they plow, prune, weed, or harvest our food. From field to studio, the sketches are the roots of my artwork that gradually evolve in the form of shaped, routed, and painted wooden panels. These four or five foot tall mural panels become the workers, men and women, bending, stooping, or stretching to harvest our food. I am grateful for my community's support of public art that honors these workers by making their contributions visible.

Bountiful Harvest, An Artist's Journey

Footsteps begins with my Bronx roots and the development of the sketchbook habit as an integral part of my creative process. Mexico 1953 was my first sketchbook border crossing, and the journeys have continued.

An Oregon Love Story jumps to 1964 and my teaching position at Southern Oregon University. This love story evolved for the next five decades like a tree with deep roots, supporting many branches that include family relationships, consistent creative work, and opportunities for worldwide travel and research. I share my creative results in the form of exhibits, books, and videos.

Voices: Growers, Farmworkers, and the Ashland Food Cooperative is about interdependent relationships. Each voice offers a different perspective on basic issues and adds to the relationship between art and reality, deepening our understanding of artwork inspired by farm work.

Community Connections: Farmworkers Made Visible presents the positive impact of art in public spaces, not only as decoration, but also as an eye-opener to a broader community reality. My intention is to portray the farm workers and their families with dignity and appreciation for their work.

An Overview

THE STATE OF AGRICULTURE IN AN AGRICULTURAL STATE

Agriculture is central to Oregon's economy, and accounts for one in ten jobs. More than 50,000 people work in agriculture, and 30,000 are employed in food processing.

- 38,000 Oregon farms are primarily family owned. They range from small local producers to large-scale operations.

- Oregon produces 100 percent of US blackberries and ranks second in US pear production, third in strawberry production, and fifth in wine grape production.

- The Rogue Valley is the state's largest pear producer and second largest wine grape producer.

- There are an estimated 500,000 Latinos in Oregon, many of Mexican origin. Oregon farmers depend heavily on immigrant workers, who generally work for less money.

[Source: *The State of Agriculture in an Agricultural State*, Northwest Seasonal Worker, January 2015, Vol. 39 No. 1]

> The majority of hired farmworkers in the United States, an estimated one million, are Mexican.

> About two-thirds of immigrants working on US farms are in the country illegally.

[Source: *Ebb in Farmworkers Slows U.S.-Mexico Competition,* Miriam Jordan, *The Wall Street Journal,* 1/24/2015]

Bountiful Harvest concludes with the 2014-2015 panels "Transitions" and "Border Crossings." While most of the harvest panels are related to real experiences from my sketchbook, "Transitions" and "Border Crossings" are based on the inner reality and feelings of farmworkers about their lives. We all need a fair chance to feel visible, be paid a living wage, and be respected for the work we do.

–BETTY LaDUKE

Kale Harvest, 2015

1 Footsteps

Bronx Roots and the Sketchbook Habit

My Oregon "Love Story" began in the Bronx. Now in my eighth decade, I have much to unravel, especially how "No" became "Yes," and how "Yes" eventually led me to Ashland, Oregon.

My father, Sam Bernstein, a house painter in the Bronx who had immigrated from a village in the Ukraine, told me, "If you want to go to college and leave the Bronx, you will have to do it for yourself." Fortunately, I did both, and my sketchbook habit was part of the process.

Art education isn't always academic. Mine began in 1942 at age nine. My parents sent me to Wo-Chi-Ca, an interracial summer camp where Pete Seeger and his banjo were frequent visitors. The art program directors were Charles White and Elizabeth Catlett, prominent African American

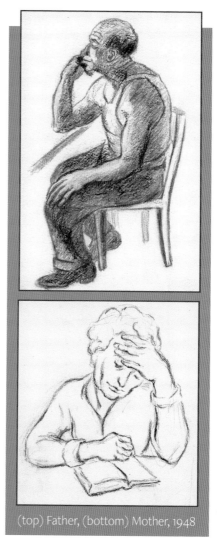

(top) Father, (bottom) Mother, 1948

1

artists. They shared examples of their drawings, mural paintings, and sculptures, which emphasized the relationship between art and community. They had also been inspired by their experiences in Mexico, especially with the Mexican mural painters Diego Rivera, Alfaro Siqueiros, and Rufino Tamayo. The large public murals created by these Mexican artists visually dignified the life and history of the rural *campesinos*, or farmers, and their survival struggles.

My sketchbook explorations began while attending the High School of Music and Art in Harlem. I ventured not only through Harlem, but also through all of New York's multi-ethnic neighborhoods and markets, and my sketchbooks filled rapidly.

My ticket out of the Bronx was on a Greyhound bus with three art scholarships: Denver University in 1950; the Cleveland Art Institute in 1951; and the Instituto Allende in San Miguel Mexico in 1953. I forgot to come home until 1956, as I wasn't sure where home would be.

New York: Newspaper Vendor, 1948

New York: Bagel Lady, 1948

Mexico: The Otomi Staff of Life

Mexico became a profound formative experience as I painted well beyond school assignments. I explored Mexico's regional diversity, pre-Colombian heritage, and all the major mural sites of Rivera, Siqueiros, and Tamayo. I also had the opportunity to meet these artists, visit their studios, and be encouraged by them.

The journey from student to artist began in 1954 when I initiated the move from the Instituto Allende in San Miguel, where my scholarship had been renewed, to independence, by setting up my own studio in a little house in Guanajuato. This was made possible by a grant of fifty dollars per month. I established a strict work routine that began with sketching my neighbors, the campesinos at the local market, or the coal miners. These sketches became the basis for my oil paintings on Masonite boards (permanent collection, Jordan Schnitzer Art Museum, University of Oregon, Eugene, Oregon).

Betty LaDuke, Instituto Allende, San Miguel, Mexico, 1953

Between 1954 and 1956 I had four exhibitions sponsored by the Mexican government, one each in Mexico City, Guanajuato, Durango, and Tuxtla Gutierrez. Prominent exhibit reviews considered me among the "new generation" of Mexican artists.

Another adventure began after I read a Carlos Fuentes novel in Spanish, *Nubes Esteriles* (Sterile Clouds). The book inspired me to go by bus to Ixmiquilpan, a major market center of the indigenous Otomi people. The Otomi still spoke their own language, not Spanish. There, a government organization, Patrimonio Indigenista del Valle de Mezquital (PIVM), was in the process of constructing one-room schools throughout their remote, arid region. I was hired, on the basis of my art reviews, to paint murals on the exterior patio walls of these schools. My name, Betty Bernstein, was listed on the PIVM payroll as "Pedro Bernadino" and I was paid the wages of a *jefe alvanil*, or chief bricklayer. I never dreamed then that I would see, meet, and paint Mexican workers sixty years later on Oregon farms. All over the United States, we depend on them for our food.

My First Mural:
San Juanico School Patio, 1955

My first mural project was in the village of San Juanico, where I lived in the teachers' room attached to the school. The teacher, Rosa, and the village judge both spoke Spanish. They introduced me to the village people who lived in scattered huts. I sketched, learned their survival routine, and asked them about their hopes and aspirations. I joined the villagers at dawn, following a procession of mothers and children with clay pots suspended by rope from their heads onto their backs, walking to the river for water. Then the corn *masa* or dough for tortillas could be prepared.

(top left) San Juanico School, 1955; (top Right) San Juanico Village, 1955; (bottom left) Juana, Tapping Maguey Plant, 1978; (Bottom right) Betty LaDuke at Patria Nueva village, 1955

The maguey plant was the Otomi staff of life, a major source of daily nutrition for each family, as well as providing fiber for cloth and for roof thatching. The thick inner core of the maguey stalks could be tapped daily for *pulque,* a beverage rich in minerals that is fermented overnight. The older thick stalks could be cut and pounded to provide a coarse fiber, *ixtle* for weaving rope, or *ayates* for square sections of cloth. Two *ayates* stitched together form a bag to contain the harvest, or a single *ayate* can be a little hammock suspended from a headband for carrying babies on one's back. Men often wore *ayates* crisscrossed over their chests. These items could also be sold on market day to provide cash for the purchase of beans and corn.

Hands planting a monumental maguey plant was the focus of my first mural. A dam would soon be constructed that would change the arid, dust-like soil, where only the mesquite tree and maguey plant thrived, into fertile irrigated soil for planting corn and beans. It was important to encourage maintaining the maguey after the dam was built and the corn and beans were planted.

I was reluctant to leave Mexico in 1956, but at this time other needs were compelling: a lasting personal relationship, children, and shared community. I would always be an artist.

United States: Chickens, Daffodils and Wild Rice

Returning to New York was confusing because the drip-paint art style was in vogue. Being an "artist" meant part-time teaching jobs at various community centers in order to sustain a modest loft studio and maintain time for painting. But what to paint?

Grandfather, 1950

After Mexico, the underground subways and fast food restaurants of New York City seemed grim. I missed people's connections with their food and the soil. Gradually, life evolved and I developed surprising new perspectives.

A symbolic approach connecting life and art began to evolve with my first full time job: art director of the Grand Street Settlement House. Each age group had different program needs, but I enjoyed the challenge as well as the long walk to work with my sketchpad.

En route to the Settlement House, located in the midst of the Lower East Side's immigrant neighborhood (my grandfather still lived on Cherry Street), I discovered chickens. They were scrawny, plucked and suspended from long hooks, and displayed limp in the front windows of kosher butcher shops. In my sketches, both chickens and people appeared like I felt, trapped, with life on hold. Fortunately for me, it would not be so for long.

Spring 1958, in my studio, daffodils replaced chickens, and their bright yellow sunglow suggested hope. I found hope when I met Sun Bear, or Vincent LaDuke, my first Native American encounter. He was Chippewa, from Minnesota's White Earth Reservation. He was passing through New York, and staying with my friend while returning from a Washington DC political mission. We became inseparable.

When I brought Sun Bear to the Bronx to meet my parents, they questioned in Yiddish from their limited perspective: "What is this? Not a Jew? Not a Christian? What is this?" I'm sure a variation of my story repeats with each new immigrant generation.

After working together at the Settlements summer camp as counselors (arts and crafts, and nature), we invested in a fifty-dollar ex-plumber's van. Filled with my many large Mexican paintings, some art supplies, clothing, and jazz records, we arrived eventually at Sun Bear's White Earth reservation and two-room home where his mother, Judith LaDuke, had raised eight children. She welcomed us.

For six weeks, I trudged along in the woods with Sun Bear as he hunted, fished, and trapped. Judith patiently involved me with hands-on food processing: skinning, cleaning, and cooking venison, squirrel and beaver. We made stews on her big, black, cast iron wood-fired stove that filled the kitchen.

During the fall wild rice harvest season, we drove to Cass Lake where Sun Bear's brothers and their families lived. We bought sacks of their wet rice, which we parched, then wholesaled to supermarkets in Iowa and Nebraska. En route, I witnessed the suspicion and discrimination allotted to Natives off the Reservation.

The snows came early, and I sensed the isolation that would soon engulf us, along with an arduous survival routine. I was glad we could pursue other options. I could never have imagined that over twenty years later our daughter Winona, as a Harvard University graduate and community organizer, would return to the White Earth Reservation with a vision of pride and new survival possibilities as she reconnected with her Native heritage.

Sun Bear and Winona, 1960

Winona happened for us in Los Angeles, where Sun Bear had previously worked as a Native American screen extra, falling off horses for Hollywood's film industry and cowboy heroes. We moved to East Los Angeles, where I could walk to Los Angeles State College to finish my academic credentials in art education, to qualify to teach in the public school system. Since Sun Bear's work was sporadic—feast or famine—he had time to develop a mimeographed newsletter, *Many Smokes*. He presented pow-wow information, sources for regalia supplies, and general news for the many diverse Native peoples that had been encouraged to leave their reservations and integrate into an urban lifestyle that they were not prepared for.

Meanwhile, it was almost December. Before the next college semester began, Sun Bear planned another business venture—he rented a vacant lot where we could sell Christmas trees we bought wholesale. I painted a big cardboard sign featuring Sun Bear with his Hollywood feathered headdress and the words, "Why Scout Elsewhere. Buy from Indians."

After Christmas, I found myself happy to return to the academic routine I had rejected in Mexico. I now recognized economic independence as a major concern, not only in my personal relationship, but in pursuing my work as an artist. Fortunately, I have always enjoyed teaching and igniting a creative spark for others.

Meanwhile, I was pregnant and the two grandmothers (who would never meet), each came to live with us at different times after Winona's birth. That is how I could relentlessly continue to complete my academic work. Each grandmother in her own way adored Winona, and through the years my mother kept returning. After a seven-year absence, my father finally joined her on a visit.

I had no room to paint in our small basement apartment, but I managed to draw with a needle tool on my wax coated etching plates that I brought home from college. My art focus became printmaking, a suitable media for storytelling with symbolic and mythical interpretations. In printmaking, I connected my Jewish cultural heritage with Mexico's elaborate Catholic pageantry, and eventually, a Native people's vision—a spiritual caring for *pacha mama*, mother earth.

(top) Los Marranos, 1962
(bottom) Christo Mexicano, 1961

The juggling act intensified with my first academic job: art teacher at Stevenson Junior High in East Los Angeles. It lasted three and a half years. Most of my students were Hispanic, and I enjoyed the challenge of presenting art projects relevant to their cultural background.

Winona and Cat, 1968

Meanwhile, along with teaching and family responsibilities, I continued printmaking and taking night and summer classes toward the Masters Degree I completed in 1963. More challenges—learning to drive, and then applying for college teaching jobs.

Gradually our journey spurred Sun Bear and I onto different paths, and after five years together we moved separately to the Northwest. He formed communes and guided people in the spiritual way of the Medicine Wheel. Winona and I left for Ashland, Oregon, and my teaching job at Southern Oregon State College, which lasted for thirty-two years. There we would experience another view of local food, culture, and survival.

2 An Oregon Love Story

En route midsummer 1964, from Los Angeles to Ashland, Oregon, Winona and I marveled at the sensuous mountain curves embraced by many shades of green that greeted us. In time, this personal feeling of earth energy and the interconnection of all life forms would become an integral component of my art. While Winona and I missed the ethnic diversity of Southern California and our old friends, we would soon develop new roots, routines, and adventures.

An Oregon Love Story could not have happened without my job and a special man, Peter Westigard. He was an agricultural scientist

(Left) Cow in Search of Sun, 1964, (right) Spiritual Cow, 1964

11

who also introduced us to a new view of nature and food production. But most essential, Peter fulfilled our mutual needs for love, family, and friends. He was also very interested in my work as an artist!

We married midsummer of 1965. Our meager savings provided the down payment for the construction of our cabin-like hillside home. We both agreed to a small kitchen and a big studio. Winona and I could walk to school and college. Peter had to drive through the valley's pear orchard landscape to the Southern Oregon Research and Extension Center, where he was intensely involved in innovative tree fruit research.

As an entomologist (scientist who studies insects), Peter was a major contributor to the development of Integrated Pest Management (IPM), a system for managing and controlling insect damage to fruit trees. IPM reduces the grower's dependence on chemical sprays by introducing the use of insect predators and other natural means for modifying pest behavior. IPM benefits more than just Oregon growers and residents, it also has wide international application.

Meanwhile, our family grew and our home expanded. Jason was born in 1970, but I continued to teach. In my studio, in addition to printmaking, I began to paint again, on canvas with acrylics. *Oregon Summer Joy*, 1972, symbolically portrays our relationship.

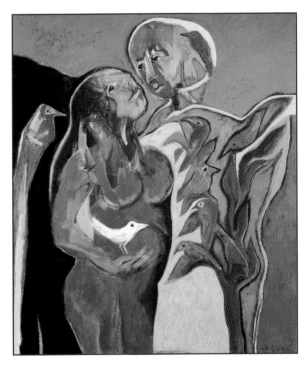

Oregon Summer Joy, 1972

"Do Something Challenging"

In 1972, I qualified for my first sabbatical from teaching. "Do something challenging," Peter said, and I did. I went to India alone for one month with pen and sketchbook. Peter also advised, "Look at peoples' connection to their environment—what they plant, harvest, and eat." I did that too, and I have never stopped. Thereafter, my annual journeys continued: Asia, Latin America, Africa and Oceania. Returning home, I juggled family responsibilities along with studio work.

(top left) India: Long Nights Journey, 1973
(center right) India: Hindu Wedding, 1974
(bottom) China: Nursery School, 1977

(top left) Jamaica: Tomorrow, 1985
(top right) Peru: Earth Mother, 1983
(bottom left) Bolivia: Pacha Mama and El Tio, 1984
(bottom right) Mexico: Between Sunlight and Shadow, 1996

I relied on my travel sketches to develop paintings and etchings on themes such as—*Impressions of India, China: An Outsider's Inside View, Latin American Impressions, Africa: Myth, Magic and Reality*, and *Children of the World*. (Permanent installation, Hannon Library, Southern Oregon University, 2006.) These non-commercial cultural exhibitions have been seen in over three hundred museums and art centers, including Chicago's Field Museum, the Dallas Art

Africa Fish, 1992

Museum, Hampton University Art Museum, and at many children's museums from Portland, Oregon to Long Island, New York.

As a mother, artist, and teacher, I was curious how other women artists juggled their responsibilities. In my travels, I began to seek them out and document urban as well as rural women's diverse art forms, especially as they related to social change. I admired their courage, as the specific conditions in which some worked included political repression and even imprisonment. I had to tell their stories! After my first publication, *Companeras: Women, Art and Social Change in Latin America* (City Lights, 1985), I continued giving visibility to their art and their stories: *Africa Through the Eyes of Women Artists* (Africa World Press, 1991); *Women Artists: Multicultural Visions* (Red Sea Press, 1992); *Africa: Women's Art, Women's Lives* (Africa World Press, 1997); and *Women Against Hunger: A Sketchbook Journey* (Africa World Press, 1997). At Southern Oregon University, in addition to my studio classes, I initiated lecture courses—"Women and Art" followed by "Art in the Third World."

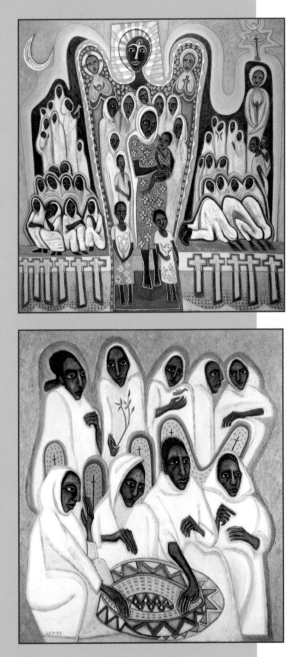

(top) Eritrea-Ethiopia: Where Have All the Fathers Gone?, 2002; (bottom) Eritrea-Ethiopia: Grandmothers Dreaming Peace, 2000

In 1996, after thirty-two years, it was time to retire from teaching, but only from teaching! My annual journeys continued, especially to Eritrea and Ethiopia during the period of peace before their border war (1998-2000) and then again after the war. This led to new painting themes — *Eriteria-Ethiopia: Where Have All the Fathers Gone?*, *Eritrea-Ethiopia: Grandmothers Dreaming Peace*, *Eritrea-Ethiopia: Prayers for Peace*, (a series of five paintings), and *Eritrea: Refugees Waiting*, (triptych). These are now in the permanent collections of the Portland Art Museum in Portland, Oregon; UNIFEM, a United Nations Women's Organization in New York City; the Rensselaer Newman Cultural Foundation in Troy, New York; and Oregon State University in Corvallis, Oregon.

Food production, food processing, and marketing have been recurring themes in my artwork, starting with my New York City market sketches. My international work, beginning with *India Spring Ritual*, then continuing with *Peru: Corn-Mothers*; *Chile Vendors*; *Cameroon: Millet Harvest*; *Mali: Fish-Talk*; *Burkina Faso: Women on the Move*; and *Eritrea: Sifting Grain and Sharing Dreams,* were enjoyable themes. However, lack of food has been a concern, as portrayed in *Eritrea: War Harvest,* and in *Eritrea: Reshaping the Land,* a painting about terracing mountainsides that had been stripped of trees (another weapon of war) so that grain crops could be planted again.

(Top Left) India: Spring Ritual, 1974; (Top right) Cameroon: Millet Rhythms, 1992; (bottom left) Mali: Fish-Talk, 1993; (bottom right) Eritrea: Reshaping the Land, 2002

Dreaming Cows

Uganda: Dreaming Cows, 2003

Dreaming Cows, a series of thirty paintings and thirty-two mural panels, began in 2003 after I joined a Heifer International (HI) study tour. My first trip was to Uganda and Rwanda, just nine years after Rwanda's self-destructive genocide. I wondered: How could the HI program of providing food aid in the form of livestock make a difference?

After World War II, HI was initiated by American midwestern farmers. In 1945, they realized that instead of shipping food aid in the form of powdered milk and biscuits, shipping cows would be a sustainable solution. Cows are a food gift that can multiply and be passed on to other families.

For the following six years, I sketched at HI project sites on five continents that included Eastern Europe and the United States. Cows and other environmentally appropriate livestock were presented to families. The program also included education about animal care and related agricultural practices, and asked for community commitment to share and pass on the gift. It was wonderful to see the difference a cow could make for a family—better nutrition, income from the sale of milk for yogurt, and manure for fertilizer. Now children could attend school, as there was income for school supplies, clothes, and even home improvements that could include electric light powered by biogas (gas produced when organic matter such as manure breaks down).

My first HI painting, *Dreaming Cows*, was inspired by a Uganda family that included five children and their cow. Since providing nutrition and teaching better agricultural practices and community responsibility develops hope and pride, I also painted related themes such as *Cambodia: Building Community Leaders*, and *Albania: We May Be Poor, But Our Culture is Rich*. A selection of these paintings, *Dreaming Cows*, became another circulating exhibition, featured first in Oregon, then across the United States at many universities and museums. I was particularly pleased when they were presented at the Waterloo Center for the Arts, the Boston Children's Museum, and the Long Island Children's Museum, where art education specialists developed interactive programs for teaching children about art, cultural diversity, and world hunger.

After donating the *Dreaming Cows* series to Heifer International for their new world headquarters building in Little Rock, Arkansas (near the Bill Clinton Presidential Library), I accepted a mural challenge for their new Education Center. Instead of painting the mural on-site, I experimented in my studio with painting on plywood panels. I sketched the design outline first, and my studio assistant Barney Johnson cut, shaped, and routed the panel. Then I completed the painting. Many of the panels were seven feet tall, and together they stretched along the wall for one hundred feet.

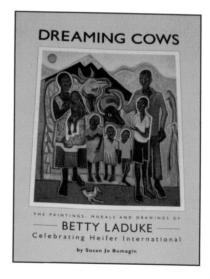

I enjoyed this new process of mural panel painting, and continued working in this media long after my HI projects were completed, permanently installed, and then acknowledged in the 2009 book publication, *Dreaming Cows: The Painting, Murals and Drawings of Betty LaDuke*, written by Susan Jo Bumagin.

My work with Heifer International led to a mural commission for the permanent site of the Farmers Market of Martinsville, Virginia. The Farmers Market organizers had received a community grant for an outdoor mural installation, and I traveled to Martinsville to sketch the activity at their bustling biweekly market and at several local farms. While I enjoyed my brief sketchbook visit, the Martinsville community is still enjoying their 2010 farmers market mural installation. It consisted of four panels, each seven feet tall by four feet wide.

Farmer's Market, Martinsville, VA, 2010

Many decades after my first experience in Mexico with the Otomi maguey, I still explore food themes, but now from a local Oregon perspective that began with a personal rite of passage. Ironically, this would lead to a new series of mural panels, *Celebrating Local Farms and Farm Workers,* and their public sponsorship and installation.

Betty LaDuke, Ashland Studio, 2011

Trees of Life: Seasons End

Stability, a rare gift in a world filled with much personal and political turmoil, was ours for over four decades of marriage. Gradually, Peter's body suffered with cancer, but not his sharp wit and spirit. I helped him through his long process of body illness needs, while we still enjoyed all that we could.

In my studio, I began a new series of seven-foot-tall plywood panels—*Trees of Life.* These three panels, each cut, shaped and routed, represent both a personal and a universal story of our life cycles: *Sunrise,* the joy of beginning and establishing a relationship; *Midday,* the challenges of raising children and questioning the future; and

Trees of Life; Sunrise, Mid-Day, Sunset, 2010

Peter's Tree

Sunset, the acknowledgement of the last season of the life cycle and the acceptance of letting go. Then we are left with another challenge—how to continue alone, but not alone? From the experience of loss and the end of our being together, a new form of "together" evolved. It began with my feeling the need to sketch a pear tree, *Peter's Tree*. This was not to be the last tree. And in the years that followed, I had new learning experiences and adventures in our local farms, orchards, and vineyards.

Summer's End, 2011

Suzi, 2011

Flowers, Spirit Food

In the midst of my long period of caretaking, a friend invited me to visit her nearby farm (Le Mera Gardens, connected with Fry Family Farm) to see the vibrant acres of flowers just prior to harvest. This dazzling eye feast became the catalyst for a new and ongoing series of mural panels, beginning with *Flowers: Spirit Food*. They were also my way of healing. I was grateful to my friends Joan Thorndike and Suzi Fry for their farm visit invitation.

I kept returning to the farm to sketch the team of six or eight young farm workers as they harvested a great variety of flowers. Joan and Suzi worked beside the pickers and I followed along, walking forwards, then backwards too, while sketching quickly. Their bodies were arched over long rows of marigolds, gladiolas, snapdragons, and miniature sunflowers, as they carefully selected only the best to cut and then secured the flowers under their left armpit. They continued this process until the necessary quotas were harvested, each bundle fastened with a rubber band. Then all the bundles were gathered and carried (almost like mothers carrying their little children), to the roadside truck, where buckets of water received them.

In my studio, a flower garden of panels kept growing, with strange titles including *Love Lies Bleeding*, a flower panel for my feelings. *Seasons End* was based on a swarm of circling birds enjoying the leftover flower seeds. One day, I particularly enjoyed the opportunity of bringing to the farm a completed flower panel of Beth harvesting snapdragons, so she and her children could see the results of my sketching, and her children could see how their mom had inspired me. A mutual respect for our work developed!

Betty LaDuke

Flower Harvest #4, 2014

Flower Harvest #2, 2011

Love Lies Bleeding, 2012

3 Voices

Growers, Farm Workers, and The Ashland Food Cooperative

The Paintings Talk Back: Art Connects

Celebrating Local Agriculture is a series of paintings that speak. They are the voices of eighty or more farm, orchard, and vineyard workers that work individually or together in teams. Their almost life size forms are cut, shaped, and painted on wood as they plant, weed, or harvest vegetables, flowers, grapes, pears, and peaches.

As I paint, I connect with Fry Family Farm workers Raul, Alejandro, Juan, Felix, Rudolfo, or Popo as they bend and kneel to harvest long

Peanut Squash Harvest, 2012

27

rows of kale, spinach, squash, cherry tomatoes, sweet peppers, chili peppers, parsley, radishes, and berries. I also connect with Suzi Fry and Joan Thorndike, who work alongside their team of harvesters— Jenny, Beth, Michelle, Laura, and Chaeli—as they arch over rows of brilliant orange and yellow marigolds, yarrow, and sunflowers, to snip, bundle, stack, and carry the flowers to water buckets before they are assembled into bouquets.

Betty LaDuke's Studio, 2013

At Harry and David Orchards and Ron Meyer Orchards I sketch and paint teams of seasonal workers, sometimes several hundred, that arrive for the annual pear and peach harvests. With buckets strapped to their chests, they climb ladders to reach the uppermost tree limbs. With forty pounds of fruit in their buckets, they climb down to empty them into bins that can hold a thousand pounds. Each worker fills six to twelve bins each day.

At South Stage Cellars Vineyard I sketch Oscar and his team thinning grapes. Later in the season I sketch and paint Marlen, Oscar's daughter, as she harvests grapes. Oscar and Marlen received reproductions of my work, and they are extremely pleased to see the original "Marlen, Grape Harvest" panel displayed in the City Hall of Talent, Oregon, the community where they live.

During the spring season at Trium Vineyard, local students Miguel and Julio carefully place grape vines between wire supports.

Midsummer, they return to thin grapes. At the summer's end, they participate in the intense harvest frenzy before returning to high school and college. In the two panels, *Grape Vine Training*, each brother carefully places the vines between wire supports. This work supports their continuing education and future dreams.

For almost twenty years I have worked as a team with Barney Johnson, my studio assistant. He routes below the surface outline to designated depths (shallow, medium, deep) before I apply many layers of acrylic paint mixed with sand. We've completed many projects: thirty-two panels, *Dreaming Cows,* for the Heifer International Education Center in Little Rock, Arkansas (1996); four panels, *Farmers Market,* for the farmers market in Martinsville, Virginia (2008); and twenty-six panels, *Celebrating Local Farms and Farmworkers,* for the Rogue Valley International Airport in Medford, Oregon (2012) and Portland International Airport, Portland, Oregon (2015). We are particularly proud of our airport installations!

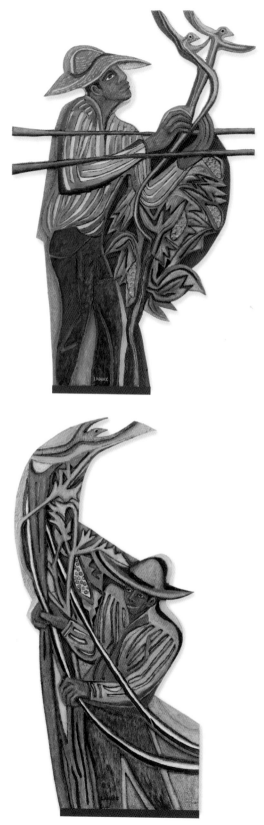

(top) Grape Vine Training #1, 2013 (Model: Miguel); (bottom) Grape Vine Training #2, 2013 (Model: Miguel)

Harry and David: Orchard Harvest, 2012

Sometimes in the orchards, as workers climb ladders and empty buckets into bins, they pause to glance at the sketches I make of them. Some approve, "Que bien!" Some wonder, "Why not a camera for better, faster results?" I enjoy our brief dialogues and interactions. I'm especially pleased when the panels featuring local agriculture are on public display in their communities, and the dialogue broadens from the enjoyment of bright colors to the meaning of the work that brings us fresh, local food.

Another link from farm to dinner table are our local Rogue Food Cooperatives. In addition to presenting consumers with the best quality of locally grown and certified organic produce, they also sponsor cultural and educational events and food preparation such as trendy kale, roasted chili peppers, and very berry desserts. They also make us aware that globally, co-ops represent one billion members/owners and that they support hundreds of local growers, suppliers, and food producers.

These varying voices and perspectives contribute to our awareness of the teamwork agriculture requires. Co-ops help us recognize the many hands that are needed to provide nourishment for both body and spirit.

Joan Thorndike: Cut Flower Grower

What I've loved about Betty coming to our fields, is that, for one thing, she's outside eyes looking at what we do every day. She started drawing and painting the people that I see every day in my workday, and they came to life.

Simultaneously, there was conversation on the radio about immigrants in this country, and immigration bills. I want to make it clear that, while I'm speaking specifically about Hispanics coming into the United States, and they have come to do all sorts of careers, the nerve that Betty hit, for me, was that she brought to life the agricultural workers.

Earth Cycle, 2014

LADUKE

I'm a flower grower. I've been farming for twenty-two years, and over the course of that time, Fry Family Farm and I have found it difficult to find long-term employees who will show up every day to work our fields. We actually have a lot of women flower pickers. Our pickers are primarily Anglo women. But you can't pick flowers if you don't have field workers.

Someone has to till, plant, weed, and water. Someone has to be there every day, to make ten acres of flowers productive. These people are all Hispanic. They show up at six thirty in the morning and leave at four o'clock on the dot. They take lunch at one o'clock until two. They never whine, never say, "I can't be there tomorrow, because I don't feel like it," or "I have to go do something else." They just show up. No drama. And it's a wonderful thing to work with people like that. And they're very loyal. And I love that we're a team. I love that

Spring Planting, 2012

my pickers and our workers need each other. Their favorite line when we come to work is "Tanta flores, Juanita. Mucha flores. So many flowers Juanita. We love having lots of flowers for you."

In the news it was all about numbers, the numbers of immigrants coming in, and stealing jobs. There was never a face to these people, to those numbers, and Betty gave those numbers a face. When I look at the art that Betty has done of our farms, I see Sylvia, Chaeli, Beth, and Suzi. I see Mr. Raoul, Alex, and Chevo. Then I realize those are all the people I work with. That's what I want the United States to know, the politicians to know, that they are part of us. They are part of our community, and they're as imperfect as the rest of us. In many ways, better than some of us!

I would love for Betty's art to travel this country, to be shown on television. When

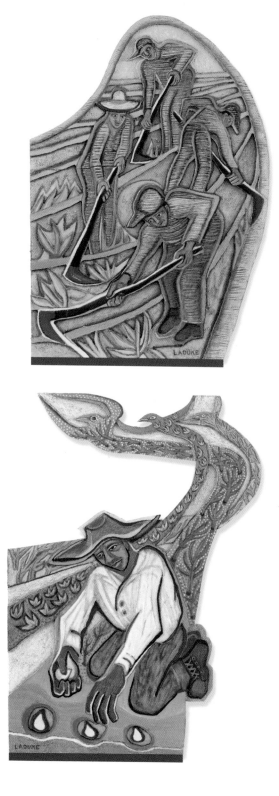

(top) "Limpiando" the Weeds, 2012
(bottom) Planting Gladiola Bulbs, 2012

the newsreel is coming through, and they're talking about "the wall," or immigration reform, I wish in the background that her imagery was going by, because that's what makes it real. I think that her art would bring to life a news report, and maybe change minds.

When you talk about numbers with no names, and it's just a report, a person can remove themselves emotionally from that. But Betty has made the food that comes to our tables a relevant point. You can eat, and you can have flowers on your table, because those people in those paintings are real. They're on our land. They're in our country. And they make it possible.

Betty asked me once, "Why organics?" When I started farming, I had a three-year-old and a five-year-old. I started farming because I needed to work, but I didn't want to leave my children behind. That's not why I had them. So by coincidences of the universe, I ended up on a farm, and could bring my children to work every day. It was immediately evident that this had to be an organic production. The first employee I had also had a two-year-old and our children were going to be running in those fields. Even if I had an employee who didn't have a child, I would still want him or her to feel unharmed.

I belong to a National Association of Cut Flower Growers, and I try to go to an annual conference. Twenty years ago, it was unbelievable what some growers would say was okay to do. There were some cut flower farm owners who said, "Of course I spray, but I don't get in there. It's my Indian workers. Or it's my Ecuadorian workers," like they didn't care. I kept thinking "Did I hear that right? Isn't this a fellow human being?" So, there was just no question that I would be an organic grower.

I wholesale to flower shops. That's my primary market, and I always invoice everything and state, "These are organic flowers." When people stop to think about it, they say to me, "Well, why organic?

Why does it matter? You're not going to eat it." It matters because it's my job not to deplete the soil on which I'm growing my flowers, so that the next person, who might want to grow radishes or grapes or flowers, doesn't have soil that's lifeless. Why do I get to use it, but not the next person, or not the next generation?

I feel very strongly that our legacy as farmers is to leave the soil in good condition, so that there's continuity, so that birds, bees, worms, and small children can be there without fear. It's also a much easier way to farm, and a happier way to farm. There are weeds. Yes. Every time people come to our farm, I say, "The first thing you're going to see is weeds. I'm not apologizing for them. They're part of how we work, and we know how to manage them." Perhaps when Betty came to our farm, it might have been shocking to wade through waist deep weeds, but they were in crops that we were done with, spring crops, and it was summer. So we just let them sit. The bees will go in there, and the insects will nest. It'll be fine. We'll be back at the end of the year.

I like for organic products, whether they're flowers or food of any kind, to be as good if not better than "conventional." I feel that word has been hijacked. We should be the conventionalists. That's the way it used to be. The organic movement made a mistake, for a long time pricing organic products very high and then giving out a mediocre flower, mediocre food. Yes, these peaches are small and they have bug holes, but they're organic. No, I'm sorry. They should have neither of those things. They should be a beautiful, juicy, wonderful peach, like the paintings that Betty does. There should be no excuses for organic growers.

Beth Wismar:
Working My Dream Job

I'm from Cleveland, Ohio. My mom didn't have the green thumb, but both my grandmas grew their gardens, tomatoes, and certain flowers. I studied conservation and geology at Kent State University. Two and a half years into it, I was tired of being in a classroom, so I traveled out West. I remember coming over the Siskiyou Mountains and feeling like I was home. I thought, "I hope to one day have my own farm here." Ten years later I was living on a farm and lucky enough to start working for Suzi Fry at Fry Family Farm and Joan Thorndike at LeMera Gardens.

Now that I see what they do, I don't have any desire to own my own farm. They work from sun up to sun down. There's really no down time except for bed. It takes a lot of work to run the farm, keep all the employees in line, and organize everything and all the markets. Right now I work six days a week, at least eight hours a day, and I have two kids. Life is full. Someone else can run it. I'll work.

GREENHOUSE STARTS

In January the greenhouses are where we start all the seeds for our flower fields and vegetable farms. We are mixing soil there, filling pots, and planting seeds. When they get a certain size, we're transplanting into bigger sized pots. Right now we have six greenhouses that we fill all spring long with plant starts that we then will sell at the food granges cooperatives and markets. That's our livelihood for the spring till the flowers start to grow. About April or May, we start doing some cut flowers. We have five farmers' markets a week and we're also shipping flowers to Portland. We do that till the end of the season.

FLOWERS: SO BEAUTIFUL AND DIFFERENT

It's nicer to pick flowers that are taller because then you don't have to bend over as much. That's a benefit. The sunflowers and zinnias and maybe things with thorns are not so nice to pick, because they're scratchy. At the end of the day you end up with rashes and itchy, but it's hot so I don't want to wear long clothing in the fields. Over all, I don't have any complaints; they're all so beautiful and different.

That's really why I like this job. In the spring we do greenhouse work for almost six months, and then we do flowers for another five months and then we have a little down time and cleaning. It's not going to the same job day after day all year long. There are some changes throughout the season. I really appreciate that and being out in the different seasons and temperatures. Every day I see the sun rise and set, and I appreciate it all. I've been there for ten years. It doesn't get old. Even today I looked up and the sun was shining, and all the colors of the flowers, and the barn in the background . . . I even took out my camera and took a picture.

Hollyhock Harvest, 2011

(Left to right) Joan Thorndike, Jenny, Beth, Suzi Fry, Sarah, and Cecely, 2012

ADJUSTING TO THE ROUTINE

It can take quite a while for a new person to adjust to the routine. I think a lot of people have this fantasy vision that they're going to pick flowers, and it's beautiful and easy and clean. They're surprised when they get out there. It's vigorous, it's repetitive. There's weeds, mud, bees. It's not as glamorous as one would think. Some people can stick with it and others say it's not for me, I'll finish out the season, but I didn't know it was so tough. We are out there for maybe five hours a day picking. Then we're in a small barn for four to five hours making the bouquets. It's a long day on your feet and a lot of female energy in a small room. I adjusted. I like it.

We use little hand clippers to cut the flowers. Between the repetitive greenhouse work, and going out to the flower fields and cutting, we constantly use our wrists and hands. A lot of us complain that we have pain and numbness in our hands. Suzi tries not to let us know if something bothers her. She pushes through. It's amazing. She does everything we do, and we're thirty years younger than her. She's tired in the evening. I tell her, it's okay. She's been farming like this for twenty-three years.

WORKING MY DREAM JOB

I definitely feel blessed that my children are being raised on a farm, in this atmosphere. Even when they go to school, and they have to write papers about what they did this summer. A lot of times they are writing about what happened on the farm, or that their mom works on a farm, and they go with her.

I'm working my dream job. The pay may not be great, or the long, hot days in the sun, but I'm very happy and there's really nothing I'd rather be doing.

Suzi and Steve Fry: Fry Family Farm

Suzi: In 2010, I remember Betty coming out to our flower and veggie fields to sketch us, and all of our people. But she had a hard time with Stevie, because he wanted to be sketched on a tractor. She wanted "hands in the dirt" people, and we have many "hands in the dirt" people.

I didn't really know Betty before that, but we were like a perfect match. She felt really at home in the fields, and it was really comfortable for all of us having her. At first we thought we might have to stand and wait for her to draw us, but she would just follow us around with her sketchbook, and we just did what we did.

Cherry Tomato Harvest, 2012

Steve and Suzi Fry, Michelle, Joan Thorndike, 2014

When she first showed us her sketches, they were very rough and I said, "Oh, I wonder what this is going to turn out like?" But as they progressed, we were really thrilled. Then we introduced her to some of our Mexican workers, and she was really excited to start sketching some of the vegetable crops, strawberries, raspberries, blackberries, beans, and winter squash.

Steve: My first impression of Betty was that she brings more than just the paint and color to her work. She brings a spiritual side that resonates with me. I don't understand why she can't do that with tractors and implements that actually make this stuff happen. Tractors have a spiritual side also. They have an essence that she can bring out. But it's the spirit of the human being that she captures in her artwork, how humans and plants work together and feed each other. All her work has the earth in it.

The workers we have come from Mexico, the State of Michoacan that has an agricultural base, so they know what they're doing. We just have to guide them in the way we do it. I've had the same employees working for us for twenty years. It's a great thing for us, as we can grow our business. We know that people are in place doing what they have to do. The way they relate to the plants and the work is the trust and the honor that they show us, and themselves too.

Suzi: The two field workers that started with us brought a lot of their other relatives, their father, one of their sons, their uncles, their cousins. So it's like a family out there. Sometimes we joke that it's the Ramirez family farm, rather than the Fry Family Farm, because we really would not be able to do what we do without them. And they work really hard for us, and we're very, very thankful for them.

Yarrow Flower Harvest and Bird Nest, 2014

Radish Harvest, 2014

Green Bean Harvest, 2010

Steve: That typifies us as a family farm. Fry Family Farm, but it's bigger than just Frys. What we do resonates in our community, as we're bringing in an organic food product that people love to eat. It nourishes their bodies, their brains. What Betty does nourishes our senses—the colors, the sensual aspects of people picking flowers, fruit, and vegetables. How can that be romantic? But you look at her artwork and that's just what it is. It's the essence of human life in the agricultural world. She really nails it down.

Suzi: I've also talked to the people that work with me, the women in our Hispanic crew, and I'm very thankful, because the work that they do doesn't really bring them a lot of recognition or people giving them thanks. So putting them into art and having them up in the airport and in public displays gives them pride in the work that they do. They have told me this. They're amazed, and they feel really good about it.

Raspberry Harvest, 2011

Strawberry Stringers, 2012 (Model: Sr. Raul)

Steve: We've been farming in the Rogue Valley for twenty-four years. We were farming before that down in Santa Cruz. And it's become the thing that we do, and that's all we do. So we're very passionate about our farming.

Suzi: We do organic plant starts for our farm, and also for other people who want to grow their own vegetables.

Steve: We have a really nice nursery, so we produce a lot of plant starts. Everything we do is certified organic. That's what my parents knew, and that's what we've always known and trusted. Now as time has evolved, we are being threatened by a new pest that's come in, the GMO pest—Genetically Modified Organism.

A lot of people say, "Well, that's wonderful. That will save the farmers a lot of work. That's great." The problem is that pollen will spread out all over the valley, and contaminate organic seed. The difficulty is, if it contaminates our seed, they own the patent on that gene pool. They can say,

Strawberry Harvesters, 2011

"You can't sell that seed, because we own it. We have the genome that you're trying to sell and it's a patent. You can't have it." So as it goes into barley, wheat, and continues on, a few companies will own the patent for all of these seeds and wipe out the organic industry.

Suzi: Hopefully a labeling bill will allow people to know what's in their food, so they can actually chose to have GMOs in their food, or not. I think it will make a big difference if people can actually see what is in their food.

Raul Ramirez, Fry Family Farmworker: This Is What I Like

Strawberry Harvest, 2010

My life is a story you can make a book or even a movie out of. My real father and my mom split when I was three months old. Then my mom met another man. They were together for almost forty-five years. So I grew up with my stepfather, who came to the United States first.

In my town in Michoacan, Mexico, I heard a lot of people talking about how we can make more money working in the United States. Dollars are worth more in Mexico. My father was working in the orchards in Oregon. I told him that I wanted to come if he could help me, but he didn't want to. He said, "You were just married and if you

come, you're going to like the life in the United States and you're probably going to forget your family, your wife and kids." He was wrong, I didn't.

I got married when I was sixteen years old. My wife, Angelita, was fifteen. When I first went to the United States, I had three kids. Now we have seven children, three girls and four boys. They were all born in Mexico. For the first seven or eight years, I would go to the United States and then go back to Mexico. We're still together after forty-four years. Angelita loves kids and flowers, especially roses.

THE MAN WORKS

I have been working since I got out of school when I was fifteen years old. Workers work all the time for somebody else. My father did. My mom was at home taking care of the house. That's the way we lived in Mexico; the wife is supposed to take care of the house, and the man works. There were five boys, and I was the oldest. We went to school, but then my father couldn't afford it. We were in a private school, the notebooks and everything were expensive, so we had to quit school and work. Most of the time, I was working in the strawberry fields.

My father had friends in the United States and began working at Reter Orchards in Oregon. I got there October 28, 1978. I've been working in the United States since then.

TRADING LANGUAGES

When I was working in the orchards, there were students from Ashland Middle School that came for summer camps. They wanted to learn Spanish and in turn, they taught us English, so we're just trading languages. They came to the camps for three months, twice a week. And then they couldn't come anymore because the school program was over. They said, "If you want to learn and keep studying, you have to go to Phoenix High School." That's what I did. I went there twice a week for a couple of hours. I learned a little bit, not much. I just practiced. I can get by.

CUTTING CHRISTMAS TREES

After the pear harvest (June, July, August, and September) everything was very slow, so I went to Northern California to work cutting Christmas trees. That was seasonal (October, November, and December), but they offered me a permanent job. In the beginning I was just a worker, but those guys there didn't speak English at all. The foreman had a hard time. When he said something, I followed. By the third day he came to me and asked if I can help him. I told him it wasn't fair, because he had three or four guys that had been there for a long time, like fifteen years. But he said, "That's true, but they don't understand what I say, and I have a hard time working with them. Sometimes I tell them to do something and they do it wrong. I'll teach you what needs to be done over here." And that's what I did. I was just like a *mayor domo*, a foreman. Every time he came to me with a list of what needed to be done, I explained it to the workers. I knew a little bit of English, and he helped. I got better pay than before. I worked there for seventeen or eighteen years before my boss died in a car crash and the farm closed.

Raul Ramirez with Strawberry Stringers Panel, 2012

GETTING LEGAL

I returned to Oregon, to Reter Orchards, because they offered me a full time job where I was in charge. My father and I worked in the pear orchards, but Reter closed in 1994. My father retired then and died two years later.

A couple of my sons were working at Fry Family Farm, so I just decided to come over and work with them. When workers in the field got amnesty, I got my papers. I got legal. I became a resident.

I first applied for my family in 1991 and it took time, but in 1997 they got their papers. Then I brought my family over from Mexico. They went to live in Anaheim, California, with other relatives, because the weather is like Mexico. They didn't like Oregon seasons, the cold and then the heat. I went to visit them in California only twice a year.

One of my brothers was working at Fry Family Farm for seven or eight years. Oscar, my youngest son, used to work for Fry for a couple of years. For a while my daughter, Sylvia, worked with us at Fry Family Farm. She has three children and they live with us. My wife loves the kids, so then she moved back to Oregon.

FRY FAMILY FARM

My two sons, Raul Jr. and Popo, started working at Fry Family Farm about twenty years ago. One of my brothers was working there and Oscar, my youngest son, worked there for two years. I've been working there for seven or eight years. This little company's growing, so they need more help. Sometimes we have to work till midnight. We get Sunday off, one day to relax. Over here, my son Raul Jr. is in charge, but he works like everybody else. It's not like other places where the foreman is just taking care of everybody.

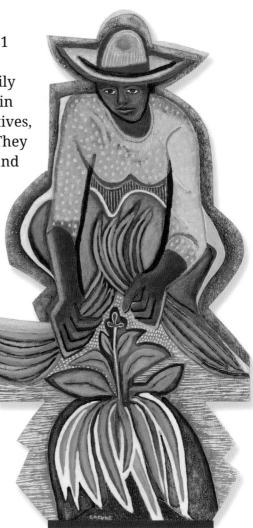

Bean Harvest, 2010

Betty with Parsley Harvesters (left to right: Betty, Raul Sr., Martin, Raul Jr.)

Suzi and Steve Fry are nice people. A lot of the time we don't see them for a week. He calls us. We all have cell phones. He knows we work the way we're supposed to. So they trust us and that makes you feel good if somebody trusts you. Sometimes we just see them on payday. We get paid twice a month. Some say we steal jobs from Americans. Working in the fields is really hard. Not many Americans like it.

RAMIREZ COWBOYS

One of my daughters, Yolanda, came to Oregon with me because she wanted to have her own business. She has a little store, Ramirez Cowboys, on Central Avenue in Medford, where she sells clothes and boots from Mexico. It's a small place, but I helped her do that. She's been there for ten years.

One day when I stopped in Yolanda's store, a customer walked in and said, "I saw you there in the airport [the mural panel installation, Celebrating Local Farms and Farmworkers]. You were picking strawberries. Now you're famous." It was good to know.

GRANDKIDS

I tell my grandkids (I have twenty-two) that they should be studying all the time, so they can make an easy living in the future. I tell them, "Don't quit talking in Spanish, because people with two languages have more opportunities to get better jobs, better pay. There are some places that need people who speak English and Spanish." I don't know if they'll do it or not.

In our culture it does not matter if you're seventy or eighty years old; they're still your kids. That's what I tell them, "If you do something wrong, I'll pull your ear." In the United States, as far as I know, once children turn eighteen or so, they can go away and do whatever they want. But not for us.

THIS IS WHAT I LIKE

I'm sixty-one. I don't feel the age I am. I enjoy farm work. My wife and kids keep telling me almost every day that I should be doing something else, because this is really hard work. But I told them, "This is what I like." I like to be in the open, in the sun and the rain, the cold and the heat. When I'm sweating I feel good. If it's cold, I also like it.

Some guys work in the fields because they don't have anything else. My brother told me that I shouldn't be here. He said, "You should go someplace else; you have a license, you have papers, you can understand English. This work should be for us. We don't speak English or have papers. I don't understand why you're here." I tell them, "I do this because I like it."

Parsley Harvest, 2014

Sometimes Steve Fry sends me to help sell produce at the Ashland Farmers Market. One lady said to me, "We really appreciate what you're doing. I know that sometimes you have to wake up early in the morning and pick all the produce you sell. We really appreciate it." It made me feel good to hear that. Others don't think about it. I think that's life.

Michael Moore:
A Bottom-Up Grape Farmer

Grape Harvest, 2012
(Model: Marlen)

For twenty-five years, I was a documentary filmmaker. That was my life in California before farming. When I came up to Oregon, I very abruptly had the responsibility of managing our family vineyard, South Stage Cellars, thrown on me. As you can imagine, there were very few transferrable skills from filmmaking to wine grape growing, and I had to learn everything on the job.

I started in March 2008, right before the growing season, when everything happens. I didn't know anything. I didn't know how to sell grapes, how to spray. I didn't know any of the steps, so I turned to my crews.

We got together and I said, "Okay, you guys have to teach me my job. I don't know my job." And that's what everybody's done for me. We have hundreds of years of rich institutional knowledge, and all I had to do was ask. Everything I know about farming I've learned from Oscar, Carlos, Antonio, and all the guys. Everybody's also been teaching me Spanish.

That is how every farm in America should run. It should be "bottom-up," because these guys are in the field. They see everything. I think we're probably the only farm in Oregon, maybe on the West Coast, that is a "bottom-up" farm.

Grape Harvest, 2012 (Model: Arturo)

I know that Oscar can feel the plants, and it impressed me so much, how he has a relationship with nature. He always has this. It's very special. He's supervising this group of over eighty workers. Oscar is someone incredible; the work that he's done in these four years, the appearance and health of the plants, is incredible. He has such a knowledge of plants. It's supremely important to observe the plant, to feel what it is saying to us. The plant always tells us what it needs. Not everyone in the world can understand what it is saying. Oscar does.

There's also a political angle that is really interesting. Everybody screams about jobs being taken away. This is work that Americans don't do any more. At harvest, over the season, we'll have 150 people

come to pick. We don't have a single person who is a naturalized citizen. Not one. With all our crews, in twenty-five years, we have not had an American come look for work on the farm. Jobs being taken away is a big lie that everybody is being told. There would be no food production if it weren't for Oscar and all the people that are working across the state, and across the country.

It's one of the hugely hypocritical things about our society. We deny. We threaten. We intimidate. These workers can't go walking around town. They are afraid of getting picked up. And yet, we are completely, wholly dependent on them for our food supply. I honor Oscar. I honor all these people who are helping to keep this whole giant section of our economy thriving. It wouldn't be done without them, and instead of appreciation, they get threatened. They get deported. They get intimidated. This hidden underbelly is a disgrace.

Personally, not thinking from a political angle, I am extremely grateful because I get to work with Oscar and our crew of amazing people every day. I wish that everybody could have the experience of stepping into this world, and seeing the people for who they are, and seeing what they do, and appreciating them.

If you're growing vegetables, they go to market and everybody eats them. You don't think about the producer. With wine, the winemakers are the *rock stars* of this industry. Everybody loves the winemakers. They get to do the presentations and the talks, and they always have people crowding around. But I'll tell you this: wine gets made here in the vineyards by Oscar's doing. And it is a zero recognition, zero appreciation kind of job, except for people like me, who actually speak the truth about where wine gets made.

When winemakers come to visit us, I always make a point of introducing them to Oscar and the crews. These winemakers also realize, in their own way, that their whole livelihood, what they're producing, is dependent on every pass that the workers do. Every pass adds up. It's cumulative work throughout the season that ends with the best fruit you can get. The winemakers realize that the care and attention the crew is putting in is what's making the product as good as it is. That's what winemakers are basing their reputations on.

Laura Lotspeich: Grapes—Then and Now

TRIUM VINEYARD: LAURA, KURT, AND DUSTIN LOTSPEICH

A hundred years ago, if you grew up on a farm, you knew that you had a job the rest of your life and for your children as well. Now, kids grow up seeing how hard their parents work, and kids don't want to work that hard. It doesn't matter if it's pears, grapes, or row crops, it's very labor intensive. Farming is high risk, so the next generation doesn't want to deal with that. Some come back. Dustin (we have two children) went off to college and came back and said, "Yeah, I do want to do this!"

Dustin has done a great job in the vineyard this year. All the fruit is sold and all the winemakers are very happy with the fruit that he's produced for them. I'm very proud of him. It feels really good to have the next generation involved, invested, and taking a lot of pride and ownership in what we do.

Kurt (my husband) and I bought the Trium Vineyard property in 1989, and planted our first five acres of grapes in 1990. At that point, we were working with one winemaker. He bought everything that we grew on that five acres for the first seven or eight years. As we expanded our plantings, we started selling to other winemakers and other wineries. Over the years, we've worked with more than twenty different wineries. It has educated us about what the winery is looking for. I'm always happy when the winemaker wants to come out to see the vineyard, look at the grapes and be involved in the decision making processes. That way they know there are not going to be any surprises for them when the fruit gets to the winery. That's always a good thing!

FAMILY ORIENTED

We try to keep it family oriented. During harvest, Kurt drives the tractor, or Dustin or I. Whoever's not on the tractor is involved in supervising the picking crews. For many years we tried to harvest on weekends so that people that had other jobs during the week could come and pick on weekends and make extra money. They would bring their kids.

That's how Julio and Miguel got started working with us. Their parents, Jose Valle and his wife, emigrated from Mexico into California, then moved to Southern Oregon. Julio and Miguel started school here, so it's probably twenty-some years ago.

Jose and his wife came to pick, and they brought the kids with them. The kids helped the parents haul the buckets. Over the years, the kids started picking as well. Then Julio (the older son) wanted to work during the summers, so he and Jose both worked summers, and then came back for harvest. It was interesting to watch the evolution. Jose (the dad) had kind of been the leader, but his English skills are not as good as his son's. So Julio moved into the leadership position, interacting with us. Then Miguel did as well, and Jose and his wife fell into the background a little bit.

I think Julio worked with us at least ten different seasons, so the first time he was out here, he was probably in the fifth or sixth grade. The last year when he was working with us, he was in Rogue Community College (RCC). He was studying drafting and auto mechanics. Now Miguel is at RCC as well.

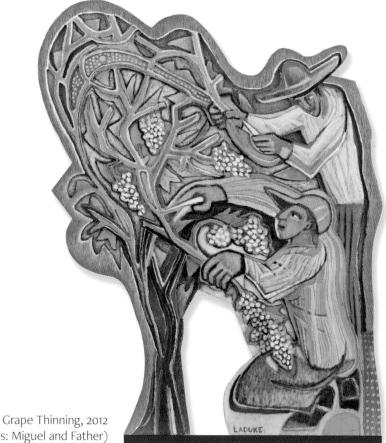

Grape Thinning, 2012
(Models: Miguel and Father)

There's another family that started with us when their kids were very small. I was concerned about them even being here, but the kids were very conscientious. They stayed right with mom and dad all through junior high and high school. Now both of the kids have graduated from college. They harvested with us every year for fourteen years. It was really nice to watch them grow up as well. The dad was also working at Amy's Kitchen, and he was an incredibly hard worker. He had worked in the stockyards before, and then in the butcher shops, and had amazingly fast hands. It was just amazing to watch him work. That was close to twenty years ago when he started with us, and he's retired now. His health has deteriorated—because of all the hard work, I'm sure.

Peach Harvest #1,2,3,4,5, 2013

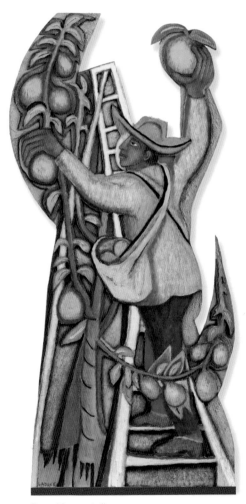

Pear Harvest #1, 2012

Some parents saw that without education, their children would be farmworkers for the rest of their lives. One family had picked every harvest day with us the whole fall, and the kids had worked really hard. The last day we were picking grapes, the daughter said, "Today we're picking for us." I said, "What do you mean?" "We helped our parents all fall with picking. Today, everything that the family picks—my brother and I get." That was the reward that their parents could give them for supporting the family. I think the first year they did that, the boy bought expensive tennis shoes. The daughter bought clothes. For four or five years, I saw what the kids were spending their money on changing a lot. She put it into tuition money for community college. He put it into sports camp. I saw the kids growing up and saying, "I want to spend this money on education, and on making our lives better."

WOMEN IN THE FIELDS

For the most part, the Latino families that have worked with us have been amazingly trustworthy, hard workers, and dedicated to doing a high quality job. When we first started the vineyard (when my kids were in grade school), the mothers of the other kids in school thought that it would be glamorous to work in the vineyard with the plants. Most lasted a day or less, because it is very hot, sweaty, dirty, hard work in the summer. It takes a fair amount of upper body strength to move catch wires and move the canopy, arranging the canes. Most women don't have that upper body strength. So the women that have worked with me over the years in the vineyard are kind of the exception. They may have started early in life doing hard work, and learned how to pace themselves. For the most part, women in America don't know that. The Latina women that work in the field have developed those skills right along with their husbands.

Pear Harvest #2, 2012

EVOLUTION FROM RADIO TO CELL PHONE

Over the years, it's been interesting to watch the evolution from transistor radios tuned to Mexican music stations, to iPods, to cell phones. But you do still get that yelling back and forth across the rows, people singing, giving each other a hard time, telling jokes, and planning family get-togethers. That does keep people going. There's a camaraderie that happens, and to some extent, a competition.

Grape Harvest Frenzy, 2012

Especially during harvest, they'll give each other a hard time, "You've only picked ten buckets. I've picked fifteen!"

For us, quality control means full buckets and clean picking. Sometimes you have to go back and remind the pickers about quality, because they'll get in a hurry to catch up with each other or pass each other. But for the most part, they laugh about the competition.

Matt Borman and Harvesters, 2014

Matt Borman, Harry & David Orchard Operations

As director of orchard operations at Harry & David, I really do enjoy finishing a harvest every year with the help of some great people. Harry & David is unique because we not only pick pears and peaches, we also know both the people who harvest and the customers themselves. We want them both to come back.

I graduated University of California, Davis, and was farming walnuts for my family in the Sacramento area. Then I worked for a hybrid seed company for about four years. My wife's family has been in the Rogue Valley since the 1800s, so we came to be close to them. Harry & David offered me the only real agricultural job in the Valley at that time, field supervisor, then I was a horticulturalist for about ten years. I was responsible for irrigation scheduling, pruning, pest control practices, fertilization, quality and maturity testing, and now orchard operations.

A COMPETITIVE MARKET

It's a competitive market for people with the skill set that we need to harvest our agricultural crops. Harry & David has a very progressive stance on how we care for these people. We need their help and we want to invest in them as well.

To bring in the harvest that we have, we'll hire about 320 professional harvesters. Most come up from areas like Central California, down near Arizona, and into Mexico. The relationship has been established for a long time, through word of mouth and the experience that workers have here. We have an ongoing communication with them throughout the year. We send them postcards, make phone calls, and send letters. We say, "We're still here. If you're wanting to come up, we'll be in these locations at these times during the year to talk to you about it or to arrange your employment." It's hard work, and it's a long way to come up to find that it's not what you expect and it doesn't benefit anybody.

RETAINING WORKERS

This year (2014), 60 percent of the workers returned from last year. Some need a year or two off to do something else, and then they come back. The actual number of new employees is roughly only 20 percent.

We have a group that on average is middle aged, but by expanding our recruiting, we are getting some younger people to come up and pick for us. We have multiple locations and we can house close to 390 harvesters. Right now there are only about 270 in our camp facilities, so we only utilize three locations. Airport Labor Camp, Hollywood Labor Camp, and Modock Labor Camp. We have a great cooking staff here that does a wonderful job.

Because we just have one variety of pear, Royal Rivera, we have a very small window to get everything in. From the day the harvesters get here to the day they leave, we do a six day a week schedule. Physically, harvesting pears is tough. We don't go longer than eight hours a day. If the workers maintain the standard and keep the quality, they can make extra money. We call it "rate-plus." There's an hourly, plus a bonus. If they stay for the whole harvest and if they do extra production, they get extra money to add to their hourly rate. Some of these guys make seventeen to twenty dollars an hour.

ORCHARD OPERATIONS: MOTHER NATURE CHALLENGES

Pear Pruning, 2013

There's a lot of guess work in trying to come up with the right answer every year. Scheduling! Making sure the pears are ready to go before we start harvesting. That's one of our biggest scheduling challenges. Mother Nature can change the day you start. You have to communicate with these guys. We need to meet the harvesters and bring them here. We have to predict when we can start. If we miss that date, and we wait too long, we lose time in harvesting quality. If I guess wrong and start too early, these guys just stand around, and they don't like that.

We have one month, and that's if the harvest isn't late. We've had years where we didn't finish harvesting until mid-October. We're always just sharing in the battle to outwit Mother Nature every year.

There's a lot of camaraderie in the group when you finish; that goes from our equipment manager, to our facilities manager, to our senior supervisors. They are here day in and day out, working with the guys in the field to make sure that from November 1, when we start pruning, until we finish harvesting in the fall, we have what we want.

ORGANIC PEARS

The first place to start protecting workers is by being responsible in the spraying program, so we minimize the use, if possible. We initiated sixty-five acres of organic orchards. They're not terribly productive for us. We struggle with it, but it's allowed us to learn about the type of organic materials that could be effective, not only in our organic program, but in a conventional program. We utilize those wherever we can. There are a lot of organic materials that we can apply into our conventional block to try and handle the pest problems as best we can before we end up using the things that are conventional. It seems like the most responsible way.

I consider us more sustainable than organic. Sustainability really has to do with trying to maintain a system that's inherently out of balance, because it's a monoculture. You can't grow 340 acres of the same tree and call it balanced. I think of it like a beach ball—you're just trying to keep the balance in the air.

INTEGRATED PEST MANAGEMENT

Fighting pear disease and blight by walking the fields once a week from March to October is a pest control program to be proud of. Monitoring protects everybody, from the workers in the field to the people that live right next to us, to the customer at the other end.

We reduced many of the harder chemicals by utilizing not only a mating disruption (of insect pests) program, but also scouting, spot applications, and proactive response time. We take information, collect it that day, and generate a response in the field within twenty-four hours. It allows us to quiet things down without having to be heavy handed; in some cases we only have to treat within a four-acre block of trees. If you can do these spot type applications, then it allows the orchard to heal much more quickly and benefits the environment around it.

APPRECIATION

As hard as these guys work, the attitude you find in the field is just amazing. That's the part that's always drawn me to this community. It can be 103 degrees, and you can be in some pretty bad conditions, and there's somebody singing, and somebody whistling, and they're giving each other a hard time. It really gives you an appreciation for the simple things in life.

Ron Meyer: Fruit Tramps and Pear Quality Control

Pear Harvest #3, 2012

My grandfather moved to the Rogue Valley in 1910 to grow pears. He had been a coal miner in Illinois, read about growing pears in Oregon in the local newspaper, and saw the ad by the Chamber of Commerce. So in 1910, he came to Oregon and brought the family. Out of five children, my father was the only one who took up the pear business. I received the opportunity from my father.

Lana (my wife) and I took over in 1971. We bought the place from my father at a little more than his cost. We built the packing sheds, and got into the packing business. We started with 72 acres, and now we have 115 acres. We grow 8 acres of peaches and little over 100 acres of pears. Our peaches are very famous, but only as a local commodity. To ship them and compete with Central California is very tough.

PEAR SHIPPING

Our pears have always been shipped all over the nation, and now all over the world. Thirty percent of the US pear crop is exported. Canada is the third biggest customer for US pears. Mexico is number one. They can't grow pears in Mexico very well, because it's too warm. We actually sent five loads to Mexico and one load to Ecuador last year. We have sent pears to Russia. The unique thing about this area, and the reason our pears are outstanding, is warm days and cool nights, which pears really like.

INTEGRATED PEST MANAGEMENT (IPM)

At its peak, the pear industry here was about 12,000 acres. When my grandfather moved here, there were 450 growers, and now there's about 15. Large companies own most of the orchards. I remember the Southern Oregon Research and Extension specialists, and Pete Westigard. He was working with IPM at the time, which was hard for us to accept. But now we are doing more IPM than ever before. It means less use of chemicals. You depend on predators, but you still have to do some spraying when the worms or spider mites or pear psylla become more than the fruit can tolerate.

My grandfather never knew what a pear psylla was. They came in the late 1950s. In the last few years, we've gotten the oriental fruit moth, the spotted wing drosophila, and the ground marmorated stink bug, which has a voracious appetite. A lot of technology has to be developed to accommodate these new pests. So in the interim, you have to spray with soft pesticides (pesticides that biodegrade rapidly), or your fruit will be ruined.

PEAR PICKING

Probably 60 percent of my pear picking crew will all be from one family—not only children, but cousins and uncles too. Roy Medina (IMG Roy Medina)came to us in 1981. He was an illegal alien at the time, and he's worked for us since that time, for over thirty-five years. He has two girls, and they have children and in-laws that

Pear Harvest, 2012

are working for us. Roy is our foreman, and he is now a US citizen. He's bought his own home. It's a real success story that he's made for himself by just being a hard worker, and conscientious. Second-in-command here is his brother-in-law. Roy's son-in-law and three nephews—all really first class workers—work here too. It's hard work, but now, a good pear picker can make 150 dollars a day, and some outstanding ones can make as much as 200 dollars. But harvest season lasts about six to seven weeks.

After harvest, as soon as the leaves fall off, the workers prune all winter and finish in March. We call them permanent part-time, because there are times when there is no work. After March, it's time to start spraying and some of the crew, the older hands, know how to operate the equipment.

ORCHARD HEATING

Whenever it gets down around 30 degrees, we're all out there turning on the fans and lighting the heaters. Orchard heaters have evolved. The heat protects the fruit, but sometimes in the past, the smoke was so thick that the sun was delayed from shining through. It actually made the frost last longer into the morning.

When we first started heating, diesel was eleven cents a gallon. When diesel got up to about a dollar a gallon, all of us decided we couldn't afford that any longer. So some of the growers put in overhead sprinklers, which is good protection.

FROM FRUIT TRAMPS TO THE BRACERO PROGRAM

When I was just a small child, there were what they called "fruit tramps." They were field workers displaced by the drought in the mid to southwest, mostly Oklahoma and Texas, during the dust bowl era. Those people then migrated to California. The reason they got the name "fruit tramps" was because they would start with the fruit in California, then come up through Oregon and into Washington. So they could follow fruit for a good share of the year. And then they would return to California to start the cycle all over. Well, that was working quite well until World War II broke out. Then they all went to the shipyards, making big money making ships, and left us without labor.

That's how the Bracero program started, in the 1940s during World War II. It was a contract with Mexico for our source of labor. We, the fruit growers, had a labor camp here. My father helped set that up. They had their housing, sleeping, and recreation quarters, and food was made for them. The growers would provide transportation to and from the orchard. That worked well until World War II was over. Then labor unions, led by George Meany in particular, stopped the program because they thought it was taking work away from the American labor force, which was totally false. The American labor force had gone to other things, and the people that would do the work had vanished into other careers. That transition left the agricultural industry without labor.

After the Bracero program was discontinued, the Mexicans kept coming anyway. If they were caught, they'd be shipped back to Mexico, and back in a week. That's what we lived on for a long time. Most of the labor force is illegal. Now, we have this pool of labor, but some have gone back to Mexico, to the point that we're seeing severe shortages and damaged crops because we can't harvest in time.

PEAR HARVEST

There's about one thousand pounds of pears in a bin. Our crews get paid by the bin. The whole crew used to empty their buckets into the same bin, and then we'd divide up their pay equally. Oh, did I hear complaining! So now we give a worker four trees. He picks those four trees into however many bins are needed, and he has a ticket that we punch for each bin. That's how he gets paid. If you have a part-time person and he picks the bottom of a tree, then you have to get somebody else to pick the top. You get a lot of complaining about that too.

There's three of the workers that can pick about ten to twelve bins, and make about two hundred dollars a day. We have Sylvino, a frail guy who must be in his sixties now, and he's one of the top pickers. He doesn't look like he's working fast, but he knows just how to set the ladder to reach the maximum amount of fruit from one ladder set. He'll go up on top, and pick the pears down, so that he doesn't carry a load of pears up. He knows all the tricks.

Betty LaDuke in studio painting.

We have all aluminum ladders. If we have one wooden ladder, oh the complaining you'll get from the guy that has to use it! But we once did it with wooden ladders, when we didn't know any better. When you're doing it by contract work, the workers want to go fast. Sometimes they'll ruin a lot of fruit if they're not careful. So that's our foreman Roy's responsibility—to make sure that they don't drop them in the bucket; the stems are notorious for making punctures. If they set their bucket down in the bin, and they pull it straight up, the pears avalanche out of there. We want them to put their bucket into the far side of the bin and pull it across, so the fruit just flows out. It's Roy's responsibility to make sure they do that. That's quality control!

If there's one pear left on the tree, he'll make them go back and get it. That's our foreman, he demands perfection. He's reasonable and he's fair. What happens if you let them leave one pear, it turns into three pears, and then six pears. So you just stop it at zero pears, and then there's no argument.

The only guys that don't respect Roy, and that he doesn't like, are the loafers, and a novice picker. The foreman has to work with these people to get a good job done, because the picker can ruin a lot of fruit. Just one puncture and it goes to the juice plant where you get basically nothing for it. They can make a #1 premium product into a cull.

PRUNING: RENEWING THE OLD

Pruning is one of the most important agricultural practices that we do. Roy teaches the new pruners how to prune. We try to thin out the fruitwood to what we think the tree can hold, and then we'll always leave what they call a "water sprout," a new shoot that will grow during the summer. We want to keep that fruiting branch for about five years, and then we want another branch to replace it. It takes two years to get that branch to start bearing pears. Then you want to replace an old one that's near it, so that you always have young fruiting wood. Young trees always bear beautiful, high quality fruit, and the old trees can do the same thing if you renew them with pruning.

Pear Tree Pruning 1, 2, 3, & 4, 2013

MEYER'S PRIDE

The pear industry's been cut by half. The peak of production was twelve thousand acres. We're at about five thousand now. The pear industry is starting to level out to the point where supply is in line with demand, and with the export markets that we've developed. It will continue this way for a long time, in the hands of a few dedicated people, because we can do things better! Pears are a solid business for those that are willing to take chances and stay with it. We're hoping that our son carries on, and maybe one of our grandsons.

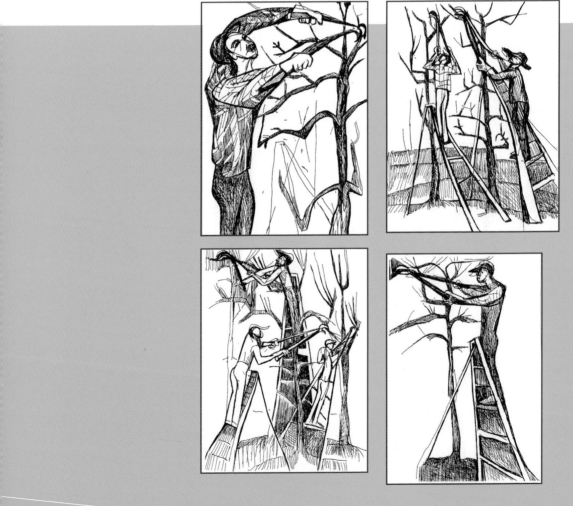

The Ashland Food Cooperative: Keeping Local Farms Strong

Barry Haynes: Cooperative Produce Manager

2012 International Year of **Cooperatives**

My parents always had a garden when I was growing up in Canton, Ohio, and my grandparents basically lived off their farm. That's always been a part of me.

After my first child was born and we were having another, I wanted to raise my children in the best place that I could find. In Ohio at that time, organic farms were very small to nonexistent, unless it was in your own backyard.

Oregon was a natural draw for me. To the south we have California and the Central Valley which provides so much food, and in the north, Washington with great apple and pear orchards. Ashland was the perfect place for us. When we moved, I was diligently looking for work and I had a couple of job offers that I didn't take. I had an interview at the Ashland Food Cooperative (the Co-op) and was crossing my fingers for this one. I got an entry-level position and was able to move up to Produce Manager.

THE REBIRTH OF AGRICULTURE

I have been working at the Co-op for nineteen years now and have watched the community demand for local produce grow. I have also been able to see local organic farms grow from a handful of trailblazers into a thriving agricultural community that keeps a lot of their produce local. In the beginning, Fry Family Farm, Whistling Duck

Farm, and Hi Ho Produce were some of our bigger suppliers. Since then it has expanded and includes: Blue Fox Farm, Barking Moon Farm, and Rolling Hills.

Fry Family Farm and Blue Fox Farm also expanded their acreage and provide more produce not only locally, but also regionally through area distributors. It has been magical to see this rebirth of agriculture and young family farmers take the next step in Southern Oregon agriculture.

Squash Harvest, 2011

NOURISH LOCAL RELATIONSHIPS

I always knew that the relationship between the Co-op and local farmers had to be mutually beneficial, and give farmers a fair price so they could farm again next year. If I treat them well, they're going to treat us well and we'll build that bond. There are a lot of produce managers who negotiate and drive prices down because they want to have the lowest price in town, but we want to give farmers a fair price. If they are not successful, we're not successful!

We'll look at the market price of the day, that's the price we see from a distributor. This price also pays a middleman. We will offer to pay the same price without the middleman, just direct. If farmers sell to a distributor, they're going to be selling for a lot less than if they're selling their produce directly to us. We need these farmers in order to continue offering local produce to our customers.

NOT-FOR-PROFIT

In a cooperative there's not just one owner sitting at the top, lining his or her pockets. We're not a nonprofit, but we're a not-for-profit. We'll retain earnings in order to keep the business going, make improvements, and put money back into the business and the community. We try to offer the best value possible. By value, I mean the best quality at a fair price. In produce we have the option of seeking out the best quality produce from the best growers with the best ethics. We set ourselves apart that way.

CERTIFIED ORGANIC: OREGON TILTH

Oregon Tilth is a grassroots organization involved in organic production. They were one of the very first certifiers who would come out and actually inspect farms to make sure they were farming organically to their standards. The US Department of Agriculture (USDA) got involved because there were a lot of different certifiers at that time, with different values and standards for organic production. Tilth has always been considered at the top of the standards, the top of integrity.

The USDA was able to bring all of that together under one standard, so that one farm couldn't be marketed as having more integrity than the other: a level playing field for all organic farmers. A lot of townspeople think, "The USDA, there goes the integrity," but I really do believe it was a good thing, because it put everybody on the same page. Tilth also does a lot of research and education, which is a side of them that a lot of people aren't aware of. They're not in it just to make money off of inspections and certification. They put a lot back into the industry through their research.

CO-OP PURCHASING GUIDELINES

It is written into our guidelines that if there is locally grown certified organic produce available, that is the first choice on our list. That's what we go for as long as the quality is there and it is feasible in terms of cost. We have very competent and capable growers in the Rogue Valley that put out high quality products offered at a fair price. We don't run into the problem of somebody pricing themselves out of the market, or their quality not being there. If it's available locally, we're buying it.

FARM TO SCHOOL: FUJI APPLES

Connecting children to the food that's grown for them to eat is important to us. Three or four years ago the Organically Grown Company based in Eugene and Portland put together a brand and a label on bagged Fuji apples that could be sold in retail stores. A percentage of the profits would be donated to local farms and to school organizations. Apples were a natural fit because they are available regionally and at the same time that kids are going to school. Apples come in the fall, and through cold storage remain available until June, typically when the kids get out of school. I was very excited about the idea and committed to donating 100% of our profits to the Farm to School Program.

COMMUNITY SPONSORED AGRICULTURE (CSA)

The CSA movement is simply brilliant. Simple in that it allows individuals to become closely involved with their organic, local food sources. Individuals purchase a share of a farm's harvest at the beginning of the season. This gives money to growers at a time when they are not bringing in any income and helps them invest in seeds and farm improvements. Farmers then have a guaranteed customer throughout their season. Most CSA's put together a box of produce based on how big of a share you bought. They deliver produce to your home or to a pick-up point on a weekly basis. It's a great way for people to connect to local farms and local produce without having to go into the grocery store and try to find where the local produce is displayed. Typically when you get a CSA, it hasn't sat in a cooler for any amount of time. It is coming directly from the farm within a day of harvest. Therefore, as a CSA member, you get fresher seasonal produce.

GMO BAN PASSES IN JACKSON COUNTY, OREGON

"We fought the most powerful and influential chemical companies in the world, and we won. A million dollars can buy jack," said Elise Higley, director of Our Family Farms Coalition, after a vote on May 20, 2014, made Jackson one of the only counties in the country to ban genetically modified crops.

The GMO ban is certainly historic for Oregon. Here, in Jackson County, the opposition (Monsanto and Syngenta) poured a lot of money into the campaign. Typically in campaigns money wins. It didn't this time. That says a lot about our local community and what it values. The community certainly puts a high importance on food that's grown in its backyard.

In Jackson County, Syngenta is the main grower of genetically modified sugar beets. Pollen can travel long distances to cross-pollinate plants of the same species. If an organic plant is pollinated from a genetically modified plant, an organic farmer can't save or use the resulting seeds because they are not organic. Contamination affects the next generation of organic crops. For us to have a GMO ban is huge and sets a precedent for the country. We're not the first to pass a GMO ban but we're one of few. It passed in a landslide.

CLIMATE CHANGE AND WATER

One thing of recent concern is the lack of water in California. Southern Oregon is also experiencing a horrible drought. The public perception is that we have water in the Northwest. There is a land grab that is starting to happen. I foresee it continuing into the future as large corporate farms move north into Oregon and Washington and start grabbing up land. That puts a lot of pressure on our small, local family farms. That's definitely a topic of concern for me right now, making sure that we continue to support local farms, keep them strong, keep their water rights whole, and prevent them from getting pushed out.

Bell Pepper Harvest, 2011

Mary Shaw: Cooperative Principles Bringing Community Together

The Ashland Food Cooperative started as a buyer's club back in the 1970s and it became a cooperative in 2003. In outward appearance it was still a grocery store, but internally, our values changed immensely, because we joined a community with principles and a business perspective that's followed by people all around the world. These principles are: voluntary and open membership, democratic member control, members economic participation, autonomy and independence, education, training and information, cooperation among cooperatives, and concern for community.

The most important principle is that the people who belong to a co-op own it. They all have an equal say, one vote. This is how a co-op is managed.

EATING GREEN

I grew up in Portland, not growing anything, killing lots of plants. Then I moved to New Mexico and lived in a little mountain village. I never ate vegetables until I discovered green chili. I noticed at that time that most people around me didn't eat kale, didn't even know

what it was, and really didn't eat a lot of vegetables, except green chili. I started researching the nutritional benefits and that snowballed. By then I had moved to Colorado. There are a lot more parts to the story, a lot of teaching about food and nutrition, and cooking in between.

I moved to Southern Oregon in 2003 and noticed the Co-op didn't have any kind of education program. I talked to Annie Hoy, the Co-op Public Outreach Coordinator, and said "You need to fix this, and I can do that for you," and the rest is history.

Chilii Pepper Harvest, 2011

TRENDY KALE

At our Co-op, I am the behind-the-scenes person. I coordinate almost all of our programs for the public. My job is to help folks who are trying out trendy vegetables find ways to make them taste good, and ways to combine them with other foods in order to create a meal, or a full recipe. I remind people that vegetables have maximum nutritional benefits and flavor when they are in season. This kind of goes hand in hand with nutrition. There's a time and season. Kale is very much a winter green, like cabbage. That's a great time to be eating kale. July is not a very good time, and there's probably not going to be local kale.

Kale Harvest, 2014

Barry Haynes added, "Because of the demand, different products are being made with kale, kale chips and lots of raw food items. They're predicting a big national shortage of kale. I don't like the word trendy, but kale is probably the trendiest thing going on right now."

AWARENESS EVENTS: BRINGING COMMUNITY TOGETHER

During our local Farming Community Week, we have the opportunity to have really dynamic, fun, and beautiful awareness events with our local produce. In October we always do a harvest festival. We

Kale weeding, 2014

feature the apples that Barry and his staff bring in. People can try them. We press apple cider, and we drink hard cider. It's a beautiful way to bring a community together.

Last weekend we invited the Fry Family Farm to come and do a chili roasting which promotes what they grow and gives people an opportunity to see how chili is prepared for use in recipes. It gave us an opportunity to share some new recipes that people can try. It's fun to have something crazy like a big ol' chili roaster out in front of the store that makes a lot of roaring noise and gives off the aroma of roasting chili. It's very dynamic.*

*Mary Shaw retired from Ashland Food Co-op after 12 years of service.

Grape Shoot Pruning, 2011

4 Community Connections
Farm Workers Made Visible

The Seed Sprouts

The seed that was planted during my first 2010 visit to Fry Family Farm continues to sprout into art that now appears in public spaces near and far. The farm workers that I enjoy sketching in the field, then recreating into mural panel forms in my studio, live in our Rogue Valley Community. While the results of their labor are visible in markets and on our home tables, the significance of farm workers' contributions are often not recognized. While in Oregon we annually depend on fifty thousand workers to hand harvest our crops (Northwest Seasonal Workers Association), many are not documented. They live in the shadows of our society. My artwork makes them visible. I appreciate their arduous work and I portray them individually and in groups with dignity and respect.

The first three panels that left my studio were based on sketches of Fry Family workers. They featured Jenny, Sylvia, and Sr. Raul (Sylvia's father), as they harvested flowers, green beans, and strawberries. I was pleased that they were selected for inclusion in the 2011 annual exhibit *Art About Agriculture*, sponsored by Oregon State University in Corvallis, Oregon.

Alejandro with Kale Harvest panel.

Venturing with my sketchbook beyond the farm into orchards and vineyards, I explored new themes. I also developed several panel sequences such as the *Peach Harvest* (five panels) and the *Grape Harvest Frenzy* (two panels). Select panels were also included in my retrospective exhibitions: *An Oregon Love Story* at Rogue Gallery and Art Center (2011), and a major retrospective featuring sixty-five years of my artwork, *Celebrating Life*, at the Schneider Art Museum at Southern Oregon University (2013). The community had a celebration with Ashland International Folk Musicians and Dancers, artists, and poets including Lawson Inada and Alma Rosa Alvarez. There was also a Sunday afternoon event that welcomed farmers, farmworkers, and families to the Schneider Museum of Art, with entertainment provided by the Ballet Folklorica (traditional Mexican dances performed by Rogue Valley young people). During this three-month exhibit, more than four thousand people came to see and experience *Celebrating Life*. My orchard and vineyard panels were perfect backgrounds for these events.

This was followed by a small but significant exhibit at the nearby town of Talent, home to many farm workers. Held at the Talent City Hall, *From Talent to Talent* also included a "Grape Harvest" and a "Pear Harvest" panel.

The "seed" continued to sprout! It was very exciting to receive community sponsorship for the permanent installation of twenty-six

Rogue Valley International Airport center section of installation.

panels, *Celebrating Local Farms and Farmworkers*, at our Rogue Valley International Airport, a two-year effort that took from 2012 to 2014. And then in 2015, Portland International Airport launched the "Bountiful Harvest" display of thirteen new panels, running from June 2015 through January 2016.

Now, southern and northern Oregon will temporarily connect when selections from my new *Bountiful Harvest* mural panels are featured at the Portland Art Museum in 2015.

The "seed" also ventures beyond Oregon as a "Grape Harvest" and a "Pear Harvest" panel will be included in my circulating retrospective *Celebrating Life*. In 2016 and 2017, they will be featured at the Brauer Art Museum at Valparaiso University in Indiana and the Paris Gibson Square Museum of Art, Great Falls, Montana.

In my studio new themes gradually began to evolve, "Transitions" and "Border Crossings." Having listened to Sr. Raul and other farm workers speak of their difficult journeys from Mexico to work and live in our Rogue Valley, I was aware of their hardships. They all wanted to stay connected with family, to have permanent work, and to become legal. Therefore, after months of repeated headlines

Transitions, 2014

about the threat to our borders, Mark Potok described how they kept coming, "part of a wave of some 60,000 unaccompanied minor immigrants fleeing staggering violence and poverty in their Central American countries or seeking a long-lost parent in the United States."[1] This led to President Obama's declaration of "a humanitarian crisis."

"Transitions" began as a painting about people suspended in limbo for an undetermined amount of time. It was about millions of displaced people from many rural areas that included Syria, Sudan, and Myanmar (Burma). I had personally seen the camps for displaced people in Eritrea, Africa, during their 2000 to 2002 border war with Ethiopia.

---

1. Mark Potok, *Back to the Border*, Montgomery, AL: Southern Poverty Law Center Intelligence Report, Winter 2014.

"Border Crossings" is a symbolic portrayal of the emotional anguish experienced by mothers, children, and families as they desperately seek refuge from violence, hunger, and despair. In my work, the mothers both embrace their children, and let go, as the future of their sons and daughters is uncertain. But the mothers continue to hope for better life opportunities for their children.

Border Crossings #3, 2015

Border Crossings #1, 2014

Border Crossings #2, 2015

Poets: Lawson Inada and Alma Alvarez

These poems were written for a community celebration in August 2013 at the Schneider Museum of Art, in conjunction with my retrospective exhibition, *Celebrating Life.*

CELEBRATING BETTY (EXCERPTS)

And through Betty's art,
we can further appreciate and realize
the common ground we share
with other humans, other lives—

infants, elders, fathers, mothers,
our human ways of community,
of reverence, of labor,
of commerce, of wonder—

and what wonder it is
for us to experience, enjoy, and sense
the varied landscapes,
temperatures, fragrances,
dreams, memories, festivities,
breezes, vegetations, waters,
sounds, creatures, muses
faces, colors, gestures,
shapes and days and nights
and all the expansive,
inclusive, mutuality

Peru: Pachamama Awakening, 2005

Cambodia: Building Community Leaders, 2006

that embraces us,
that enriches us,
thanks to Betty's art.

So now, as these walls
transform into timeless vistas
of wide horizons
and transcendent skies,

may we proceed
eye to eye
and heart to heart,

in the spirit of Betty's art!
–LAWSON INADA

Nepal Harvest, 2009

IN BETTY'S STUDIO (EXCERPTS)

In Betty's Studio
the floors
are a kaleidoscope
of color
and the walls
and easels
can barely
contain
various-stage
sketches
and paintings
of ordinary
people
 caught
in the beauty
of being
themselves:
Syrian women
Together
in prayer;
African women
carrying
a little piece
of future

Syria: Prayers for Peace, 2003

Mozambique: Vanishing Rainforest, 2006

in the wide-eyed
children
they hold
in their arms
or wrapped
around
on their backs;
A Rogue Valley
farm worker
caught in the squat
needed for the picking
of strawberries;
another
reaching
to cut a grapevine.

In Betty's
Studio
our neighborhood
becomes
magical
and is alive.
–Alma Alvarez

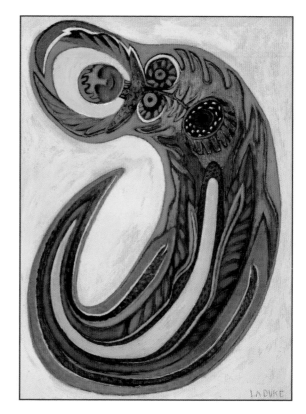

Papua New Guinea: Fertility Spirit, 1978

Children's Letters

The Children's Letters were a thoughtful and delightful surprise. The children wrote them after visiting my exhibition at the Talent City Hall. This small but unique exhibit site has select walls designated to function as a modest public art gallery so that local people experience art as they pay their bills. I appreciated the Talent Art Councils' invitation and I organized a mini retrospective *From Talent to Talent*.

In my exhibit statement, I explained how after arriving in Ashland in 1964 to teach at Southern Oregon College, I became enamored with the goats and cows that grazed at the Talent Avenue Farms. They became sketchbook subjects and in my studio they were transformed into etchings and collages.

Oscar at Talent City Hall Exhibit

In some ways the Talent "seed of inspiration" that evolved from this local experience has continued to inspire my artwork. Honoring the earth, our common home that we all depend on, and respecting cultural diversity continue to be my basic art themes. Select examples of my art were exhibited along with the original 1964 *Talent Goats and Cows*. *From Talent to Talent* also featured current mural panels "Marlen, Grape Harvest," and "Pear Harvest."

During this three month Talent exhibit I was delighted to meet with the Talent Elementary School's fifth grade class and their teacher, Sharon Kuruyama. After giving them a guided tour of artwork based on experiences in Latin America, Asia, Africa and East Europe (inspired by Heifer Internationals' sustainable community solutions to hunger and malnutrition), I also spoke of my local artwork including the "Grape Harvest" and "Pear Harvest" panels.

Then I asked the students if their family members worked in agriculture and participated in the harvest of our local vegetables, flowers, tree fruit crops, and grapes. Several students shyly raised their hands. This was my opportunity to

School children with Betty LaDuke at Talent, Oregon City Hall Exhibit

explain how we all depend upon growers and farm workers for our nutrition. Since almost everything we eat comes wrapped in plastic, we forget the source and the required hard work.

The fifth graders were intrigued by my artwork process that begins with sketching workers on location, and surprised that our local environment could inspire art. I enjoyed our interaction and was delighted to read copies of their letters written to Talent's Mayor, William Cecil. They thanked him for ensuring that art and the artist were part of their class experience at the City Hall.

I particularly appreciated the students' comments about my artwork, such as Josie's: "She captures the hardness and remarkable feeling of the workers in Talent and all over the world."

From Talent to Talent also gave me the opportunity to connect past and present, 1964 to 2014, and to interact with the community. I also enjoyed when Oscar, a worker from South Stage Cellars, visited Talent City Hall to see the large panel of his daughter, "Marlen, Grape Harvest." I wondered if connections between the artist and the people that inspire their work could happen more often.

In some ways, a large circular connection occurred. The people that inspired my art as a young student living in Mexico, are the very same people that inspire my art now. What was once very far away and different had become close and familiar.

The students shared their impressions from our time together in letters they sent to the mayor of Talent:

Dear Mayor Cecil,

Hi my name is Josie. I am in 5th grade at Talent Elementary. How are you? We went to City Hall on January 24th to see Betty LaDuke's art. We also learned that Betty LaDuke met Diego Rivera.

I thought the art from Betty LaDuke was inspiring. She catches the hardness and remarkable feeling of the workers in Talent and all over the world. I think her art is a real good thing to look at because you don't see something like jewelry or fancy people or country. She captures the feeling of workers working hard to get the food we have. I think Betty LaDuke is an amazing artist.

Sincerely,

Josie Bolstad

Dear Mayor Cecil,

Hi my name is Alex. I'm a 5th grade student at Talent Elementary. On Jan. 24 my class and I went to meet Betty LaDuke and see her art.

I really liked the themes of Betty LaDuke's paintings. It showed kids playing and people working really hard to give us the food we need. Thank you for the opportunity you gave us to meet Betty LaDuke and see her amazing paintings.

Sincerely,

Alejandro Osorio

Dear Mayor Cecil,

Hello my name is Jourden. How are you? I am happy to write this letter to you. I am in 5th grade. We went to the city hall on Thursday January 24th. We visited because we wanted to see the artist. How Betty thinks about her art. She thinks about her life. Our school, Talent Elementary, is near the City Hall. It is so fun!

Thank you very much for what you did for us. You are very kind. I love art. I am a very good artist. I think Betty LaDuke's art is great. She knows how people feel in life. I want to be like her. I want to do what she can do. Her art is the best.

Thank you.

Sincerely,

Jourden DeVey

Community Sponsored Art

After the growing presence of farm workers standing around my studio—totaling twenty-six almost life-size mural panels—it felt very lonely when they left all at once. They had been a close part of my life and work, but I was glad they were going into a permanent home, the Rogue Valley International Airport in Medford, Oregon. There they would experience many hundreds of visitors each day to admire them.

It took a long time, from 2012 to 2014, for the mural panels' journey into a public space to be completed. Their formal acceptance process began with Bern Case, the Airport Director, who visited my studio, met the farm worker panels, and then came back again with the airport Art Committee. While they were all affirmative about wanting the permanent presence of these farm workers in the airport, there was a long procedural process requiring approval from several sources, including the Jackson County Commissioners. Also, a trial period to prove favorable public acceptance was necessary. The panels could only be in their airport home, high up on the wall that stretched one hundred feet above the baggage terminal area, for a one-year trial visit before the required final approval.

I also had a request: the background wall for these farm worker panels had to be painted a very light, warm, sunny yellow color. That request was granted. On the designated day, my assistant Barney Johnson and

I delivered all twenty-six panels and a plan for their presentation sequence. Their installation by the airport maintenance staff went well, as they used a cherry picker for the panels' installation.

The farm worker panels received approval, but then came the big question: How would the artist be compensated for her work? Airport funding was not available. Then Bill Thorndike from Medford Metal Fabrications stepped forward. He is a generous businessman as well as a community benefactor who knew how to bring twenty-six individuals together. They represent a variety of Rogue Valley business and professional services as well as some individuals and families, each willing to sponsor a farm worker panel. It all happened quickly with the additional support of the Medford Foundation.

I was paid a modest fee, allowing me to give Barney Johnson a modest bonus for his incredible technical skills. In addition, the donors would receive public recognition for their contribution to the artist, the airport, and to our community.

Oregon Sunrise, 2011

From my perspective, *Celebrating Local Farms and Farmworkers* is a unique cooperative adventure, perhaps a role model for future public installations. The farm workers and their families can see themselves and their work made visible and honored as they travel and pass through the airport. This is a significant experience for them. It shows that our community honors our agricultural base and the farm workers' contribution to our local economy.

Zinnia Harvest: Morning, Noon, Afternoon, 2014

Featured Orchards, Vineyards, Farms and Community Cooperatives and Non-Profits

Le Mera Gardens
http://www.lemeragardens.com
P.O. Box 1014
Talent, Oregon, 97540

Fry Family Farm
http://www.fryfamilyfarm.org
P.O. Box 1014
Talent, OR 97540

Harry and David Orchards
http://www.harryanddavid.com
2500 S. Pacific Hwy.
Medford, OR 97501-2675

Meyer Orchards
http://www.meyerorchards.com/index.html
6626 Tarry Lane
Talent, OR 97540

South Stage Cellars Vineyard
http://southstagecellars.com
P.O. Box 1323
Jacksonville, Oregon 97530

Trium Vineyard
https://www.triumwines.com
7112 Rapp Lane
Talent, Oregon 97540

Ashland Food Cooperative
http://www.ashlandfood.coop
237 N First Street
Ashalnd, OR 97520

Author royalties and a portion of White Cloud Press sales will support cultural and educational programs for farmworkers' children in Southern Oregon through The Oregon Community Foundation.

THE OREGON COMMUNITY FOUNDATION

www.oregoncf.org

MEDFORD   PORTLAND
541.773.8987   503.227.6846

Acknowledgments

I want to thank the many people and their diverse skills who contributed to *Bountiful Harvest*—both the book and the art exhibitions—honoring the agricultural workers within our community and beyond.

The White Cloud Press team: especially publisher Steve Scholl, who encouraged me to keep writing as well as painting, and Christy Collins Medley for her innovative graphic design.

Barney Johnson: a superb Technical Assistant for cutting and routing almost 200 mural panels from 1996 to 2015.

Joan Thorndike, Suzi and Steve Fry: for their invitation to visit and sketch at Le Mera Gardens and Fry Family Farm, 2010, and for their continued support of my work.

Josh Minchow from Harry and David: for facilitating the sketching of the pear and peach harvest.

Peter Westigard, Porter Lombard, Rick Hilton, and Phil Van Buskirk at the Southern Oregon Research and Extension Center: for connecting me with Trium Vineyard, South Stage Cellars, and the Rogue Valley agricultural community.

Bern Case, Director, Rogue Valley International Airport, Al Willstatter, Airport Advisory Board, and the Airport Art Committee for their enthusiastic support.

Bill Thorndike and the Medford Foundation for organizing community sponsorship for the permanent installation of 26 mural panels "Celebrating Local Farms and Farmworkers" at our Rogue Valley International Airport, Medford, OR.

John Olbrantz, Director, Hallie Ford Museum of Art, Willamette University, and Shelly Curtis, Director, Art About Agriculture, Oregon

State University, for first exhibiting the Oregon Harvest Panels, 2011.

Michael Crane and Erika Leppman, Former Directors, Schneider Art Museum, Southern Oregon University for exhibiting "Celebrating Life," which included 15 Oregon Harvest Panels, 2013.

Bonnie Laing-Malcolmson, Curator of Northwest Art, Portland Art Museum for exhibiting Oregon Harvest, 2015, and for writing the Foreword for *Bountiful Harvest*.

Greta Blalock, Art Administrator at PDX, Portland Airport for exhibiting "Bountiful Harvest," 2015.

PHOTOGRAPHY BY

Rob Jaffe: mural panels and paintings, 1969-2015.

Jim Craven, Mark Arinsberg and Eric Rose.

Kent Romney: audio interview recordings

Stories and interviews typed and transcribed by: Sharon D'vora and Jamie Budiana.

Spring Transitions, 2011

About the Artist

Sunflower Harvest, 2011

BETTY LADUKE (American, born 1933) resides in Ashland, Oregon where she is professor of art emeritus at Southern Oregon University, having taught there from 1964 to 1996. LaDuke has exhibited widely around the United States including at the Schneider Museum of Art, Ashland, Oregon; Hallie Ford Museum of Art, Salem, Oregon; University Museum, New Mexico State University, Las Cruces; Dallas Museum of Art, Texas; The Field Museum of Natural History, Chicago; Chattanooga African American Museum, Tennessee; Indianapolis Art Center, Indiana; and the Albany Museum of Art, Georgia. Her work is represented in public collections including the Jordan Schnitzer Museum of Art, Eugene, Oregon; Brauer Museum of Art, Valpariso, Indiana; Rensselaer Newman Foundation and Cultural Center, Troy, New York; Heifer International, Little Rock, Arkansas; Portland Art Museum, Oregon; and the Rhode Island School of Design, Museum of Art, Providence. LaDuke has received numerous awards such as the Oregon Governor's Award in the Arts (1993) and the National Art Education Association's Ziegfeld Award for distinguished international leadership (1996).